D1366711

A Sense of the Morning

A Sense of the Morning

Field Notes of a Born Observer

David Brendan Hopes

MILKWEED EDITIONS

Published 1999 by Milkweed Editions
Printed in the United States of America
Cover design by Big Fish, San Francisco
Cover photo by Darrell Gulin / Tony Stone Images
Interior design by Donna Burch
The text of this book is set in Adobe Garamond
99 00 01 02 03   5 4 3 2 1
First Edition

Milkweed Editions, a nonprofit publisher, gratefully acknowledges support from our World As Home funder, Lila Wallace-Reader's Digest Fund, and Reader's Legacy underwriter, Elly Sturgis. Other support has been provided by the Elmer L. and Eleanor J. Andersen Foundation; James Ford Bell Foundation; Bush Foundation; Dayton Hudson Foundation on behalf of Dayton's, Mervyn's California, and Target Stores; Doherty, Rumble and Butler Foundation; General Mills Foundation; Honeywell Foundation; Jerome Foundation; McKnight Foundation; Minnesota State Arts Board through an appropriation by the Minnesota State Legislature; Norwest Foundation on behalf of Norwest Bank Minnesota; Lawrence and Elizabeth Ann O'Shaughnessy Charitable Income Trust in honor of Lawrence M. O'Shaughnessy; Oswald Family Foundation; Ritz Foundation on behalf of Mr. and Mrs. E. J. Phelps Jr.; John and Beverly Rollwagen Fund of the Minneapolis Foundation; St. Paul Companies, Inc.; Star Tribune Foundation; U.S. Bancorp Piper Jaffray Foundation on behalf of U.S. Bancorp Piper Jaffray; and generous individuals.

Library of Congress Cataloging-in-Publication Data
Hopes, David B.
    A sense of the morning / David Brendan Hopes. — 1st ed.
        p.   cm.
    Originally published: 1st ed. New York : Dodd, Mead, c1988.
    ISBN 1-57131-233-1 (pbk.)
    1. Nature. I. Title
[QH81.H73 1999]
508—dc21   99-24559
                                                                  CIP

This book is for Jonathan,
Rebekah, David, and Daniel

A Sense of the Morning

Introduction

I CANNOT REALLY PRESENT *A Sense of the Morning* as a book of nature loving. I have not gone camping in ten years and didn't like it that much when I did. I stop being interested in hiking when I start being tired, by which time I have probably seen enough.

If I "love" nature it is not because nature is beautiful— though, of course, it is beautiful—but because it bears witness. The witness it bears is terrible and uncompromising. Like the blow of a swan's wing or a sudden plunge into a waterfall, nature can wake us into immediate and not always gratifying awareness. Bracing and immaculate, it can take our breath away without leaving us any the wiser. Job and Arjuna shut their mouths before the essential grandeur of God, and yet their questions, at least the questions they *thought* they were asking, are not answered. Nature is not usable to the mind in its unmediated state. "Civilization" is the word we use to describe our response to that fact. We have created a second world in order to cope with the intractability, the essential mystery, of the first one.

With nature, therefore, I do not seek intimacy, but understanding, and not of it, but of me.

I used to think—I got this from the Romantic poets—

that exploration of the natural world was exploration of the Wholly Other, the sublime and unreachable, that Nature and I had nothing to do with each other, except as subject and perceiver. What folly that was! It is a separation as abrupt and unscientific as that which the more squeamish Victorians made between ape and man. I have come to believe that the difference between myself and the creatures of Terra is one of degree only, and that the balance is not always in my favor. My cats and I are all spiritual beings; I simply obsess more about it. The motivations of the wolverine and the bluegill and myself are, I think, mutually recognizable, if we could just get the vocabulary right. I used to go out looking for gods and now I go out looking for family.

I do in fact rather cast sideways glances on the too-vehement lover of nature. If a friend says from a speeding car, nodding her head toward a patch of woods between farm houses, "I love nature," I mark down in my mind never to hike with this one, never to take her very far in to the shadow of the trees. It's dangerous to be enamored, however genuinely, and yet ignorant, like a child toddling toward a crocodile, unafraid because its toothy visage wears a smile. If a friend says, "I saw a blue pool against a wall of ice," if she buttons her top button and marches grimly out into the night, I know I have found the right companion. One must love nature as the deer loves the cougar, as the dry grass loves the flash fire, not for pleasantness, but for the last part of ourselves, the culminating majesty which would just as merrily blast us into atoms.

What do we seek when we enter the wilderness? Is there anything to seek except, ultimately, ourselves? The doe and her fawn, the trout balanced in Bent Creek like a compass needle, are not identical to oneself, but are, nevertheless, allies, members of the same party. I don't mean this in a purely ecological sense, either. I would say I mean that we are connected *spiritually*, but that is hardly more specific, and bound to irritate those to whom matters of the spirit are an embarrassment. Let us say this: bird, beast, flower, stone, we are overflowings of the same inexhaustible fountain, longing for one another with the longing of separated twins. The hemoglobin in the whale's blood warbles to the chlorophyll in the mountain pine; both cry out to the star that forged their chemistry in convulsions of a vanished dispensation. We are children of the same House, the first House, and the only.

I have written a book of firsts—the first flower, first bird, first winter night on the mountain—on the faith that such things are valuable because they mark the moment when flower, bird, mountain announce themselves to the soul, bristling and stupendous with power. I wish I could live a thousand more generations, in order to have something to say about that last of these things as well. Surely my ancient soul, ready for Nirvana, or whatever the launching pad from the present sphere of creation might be, will think differently of bird and flower and mountain than this young, brash one does. Perhaps it will really mean it when it calls these things the names I now use simply as a matter of rhetoric: mother, brother, child.

The thirteenth-century Flemish mystic John Ruusbroec writes in *The Spiritual Espousals:* "Christ, the wisdom of the father, has from the time of Adam spoken to all persons in an interior manner according to his divinity, addressing him with the word, *See!*"

In this life, anyway, I think it is almost enough if I am

able to point to this and that and cry out, *See!* If that's
what you want from a book, read on. I am not really an
expert on anything, except what I have seen, and even
that I twist—knowingly and proudly—to suit the necessi-
ties of my heart.

One's deepest intuition is that the world is holy.
Whether this is a subliminal apprehension of the majesty of God or subliminal compensation for the absence
of God does not, ultimately, matter. A buttress raised by
faith and a buttress raised by despair will both hold the
roof up.

A Sense of the Morning

The Raven's Wing

O N THE ISLE OF MAN it was tradition that one, leaving the house at morning, would take as his spiritual guide the first thing his eyes lit upon. How this worked I'm not sure, except in the obvious cases of the vicar or the village idiot. How would you conduct yourself if the first thing you saw were a wren or a lichenous boulder or the gray head of a seal in the tide? What if you knelt to tie your bootlace, and saw a sexton beetle rolling its little globe of death toward the shrubbery? Would you take wing off the sea cliffs with the soaring merlin? What if the cry of a strange bird caused you to stare first into the blank blue of the sky, featureless and infinite? What if it was a cherub with a flaming sword? What if a god? What if you woke and saw the panther crouching at your side, deciding whether you were Master or Supper? Would you then be your own judge and executioner, the instrument of your own destiny?

On an ordinary morning, waking, I see a green tangle (or a brown tangle, if it's winter) of caney bushes. I don't think I want to be that. I don't know what I would have to say if I were. Sometimes it's a cat, or the Carolina wren, or the whispering sweet gum which is the largest tree in my

yard. Folk legends abound with stories of animal bodies
enfolding the souls of men: werewolves, the were-jaguars
of Mexico, the seal people of the North Sea coasts. These
are usually thought of as allegorical recognitions of the
beast within. Being a poet, and knowing the workings
of allegory, I don't believe that is the case. Or to put it another way, there is a level of intensity in the flesh and the
emotions which frightens us so that we come to think of
it as allegorical. We are unable to sustain the power of our
imagination fully embodied. We begin to analyze our vi-
sions, shattering them into component motivations and
the upwelling of ancient emotional concerns which might
have nothing to do with the real moment of the vision at
all. A vision does not explain anything that *has* happened;
it sets the stage for what *will*.

I would love to wake and take a dragon or an angel as
my guide for the day, but that does not seem quite likely.
Perhaps it is more likely not to be a thing or a creature at
all, but a quality of light, a low hum of sound issuing from
your surroundings, a pattern or a mood rather than a body.

Imagine this: You are an interstellar voyager. You left
Earth when you were very young. You've lost count of the
years during which your world has been a cylinder of hy-
brid metals, silent, cold, unimaginably swift, progressing
imperceptibly through the net of stars. But one day you
wake—or not quite wake, but hover between dream and
waking—with a scent in your nostrils, wet and cool and
dark, sweet and bitter at once, motionless as stone, quick
as rain. Automatically your mind reaches back, probing,
struggling for remembrance. Then you have it. You wake,
fully now, with a sense of the morning, starting straight
up as you did as a child, ready for the saffron light gushing

at your window. Then you realize where you are, trapped in metal and silence and starlight. But you have gained something, a possession, something internal and therefore permanent, some weightless baggage worth fully the rest of your cargo, whatever it is. The possession is memory, sense-memory, the sense of morning, that knot in the nerves you carry forever, the pearl called Home.

Imagine this: It is your own room in your own house. After troubled sleep, you wake. You survey your space, to determine why you are no longer comfortable, no longer at home. For some reason everything is changed. You are an old bird in an old tree. Something must change.

As you cogitate, night's complexities dissolve into a pure geometry of sparkling dew. Each twig, each blade of grass is edged in pulsing light. Some power has burned habitual perception away. What was green is blazing emerald. The heights arc into the sky; the depths plunge toward the bottom of the world. You have been given new eyes. You don't remember asking, or having the wisdom to ask for them, but still they sizzle in your sockets like baby stars.

Perhaps when you first woke, you saw the eye of dew balanced on the grass you forgot to mow. Perhaps, like the men of Man, you took that for your guide for the day, seeing everything fresh, with a lens distilled from the breath of a dreaming planet.

A locust tree leans past your window, as it always has. But, as in a naive painting of Eden, it wears now leaf and blossom and fruit at once. The birds of May and the birds of October jostle in its branches. White crescent moons of flowers perfume the air. Wing, keel, stigma, anther stand forth, each hair and filament etched in fire. Freed from the labor of distinguishing potential from actuality, history from present moment, the possible from the longed-for, you simultaneously feed and hunger.

O Locust Tree! you cry, believing for the first time that it will hear.

On ordinary mornings, a cardinal sings from the locust's top branch. If he did so now, the window would burst and the walls reverberate with scarlet thunder, the roof explode like paper on a bonfire.

The lover who lies beside you on the bed is almost unrecognizable for beauty and solemnity and delight— human, of course, but like the locust tree, actual and potential in one instant, spring and summer, golden autumn, diamond of winter. A fluttering of lids, a breath exhaled would shake the roots of mountains.

What are these things made of? What fire settled? What whirlwind condensed?

At last you perceive the immensity of the miracle. Waking, you saw the last pale star. That is what you took to yourself. That is what you became.

This time I mean it quite literally. The hand on the sheet beside you is made of carbon, oxygen, calcium, nitrogen, iron, magnesium, its finger brightened by a gold ring. Now, only the hydrogen bound to the waters of that body is primal stuff. At the creation of things was hydrogen, the One. To give your lover's hand indispensable carbon, a star burns through a six billion years' supply of hydrogen, fusing hydrogen nuclei into helium, fusing clustered helium nuclei into carbon, four times three, a trillion-fold each second.

Stars too small to burn carbon die, flickering out into cold ghosts attended by dead worlds. But supergiants capable of carbon fusion collapse, reignite by the pressure of compression, then commence fusing their nuclei into oxygen. Having burnt their oxygen, they once again collapse, reignite, burn sodium, collapse, reignite, whirling through the terrible cycles of fusion and collapse and resurrection until the fuel to their furnaces is iron. The star finally explodes, shucking off layers of itself like a Catherine wheel. Its cast-away matter scatters through the universe, to be sucked up by infant planets, and at last, our own, this Earth, after God knows how many generations of suns, gathering the jetsam of vanished worlds that your lover might wake embodied at daybreak.

Light elements between helium and carbon, too complex to be fully elemental, too fragile for the roaring furnaces, are nudged into existence by cosmic rays.

For elements beyond iron, not even the crucible of a star suffices. The light of the luminous bedroom clock, the gold of the ring that binds you, are born of a supernova, an exploding colossal sun in which incomprehensible force and unimaginable resistance meet head-on and, despite the cocktail party paradox, do not stalemate, but flower into the principle cataclysm of created worlds. There is nothing comparable. It is Physics throwing up its hands and abandoning its own rules, its own admittedly liberal sense of proportion. To be within a billion miles is to be snuffed out in terrible splendor. Supernovae briefly outshine galaxies. Heavy elements hurl outward from the fading wreck. These fall into suns, onto the frozen faces of unawakened planets. They rained into the trencher of the infant Earth, so that, four billion years later, they might course through your blood, eddy in and out with your breath.

Take *that* as your guide for the day.

Tell this to a suicide, if he gives you time.

Answer with this when the priest asks, "Who made you?"

～

Where I was born there are no mountains. Living in them now is like living on a strange planet, where everything must be learned new. You can't see the sun or the moon coming a long way off as you can on the plains; you wait for them to peep over the crags in their own good time. You look at the stars provided straight overhead, knowing there are others, secret ones, hidden ones, behind the black heads of the Blue Ridge. These you will not know until you move, and you will not move until you love.

I took at one point to running the mountain paths. It's chancy, but I go slow. The first thing is to train the imagination to give your ankles the heft of elephant feet, great spreading pads twisted neither to the right nor to the left by roots and stones. The next thing is to keep your eyes open. You can avoid sticks and other obstacles you haven't really *seen* if you keep your eyes open, if you let them do the work, by-passing, sometimes, your own brain. You jerk to one side, then your brain wonders why, then your ear feels the sting of a briar or a thorn passing, which might have torn you open had you waited for your consciousness to move you.

I've fallen several times in mud and leaves so thick and yielding that I wouldn't have known I had fallen, but for the sudden stop, for the altered perspective, the blue air suddenly shut down across my head like a dome. I was

looking out; now I am looking up, seeing ravens spiraling
in cobalt air. Once you see the ravens, however, you stop
running. You stand up, brush the mud off, lest the ravens
see you this way. There is a gravity about them which does
not diminish even when you notice they spend most of
their time at play, silly play, like overgrown children, tipsy
and raucous.

Ivestor Gap sizzles in a blaze of light, and there are the
ravens, like blessed spirits at play. They swoop down toward me, haul up no farther from my head than I could
jump, if I dared. I know they are black, but they flash and
sparkle in the sun, black opal, black diamond, black like
a star so bright behind the night hills it burns through and
bathes the cove in black light. The noise of their wings is
a flight of arrows, a boy switching a green wand through
the air. I had always thought of the flight of ravens as
silent; it is certain that the birds do not. It is a perpetual
singing. It is what a raven must think of as itself.

It took time for the mountains to impress me. People
would say, "Look at the mountain," and I would, but
without the emotion implied by their voices. I grew up
in a gentler landscape, not a place tourists go for snap-
shots, but one revealing beauty and intricacy at close inspection: the speckles of the salamander's back, the gills
of mushrooms, a frill of leaves. Man was born on a plain,
and in this, my sense of the homeplace, as in many things,
I am profoundly conservative. But I at least see the attrac-
tion of mountains now, the land tilted like blankets over
the knees of a giant Sleeper, the animal-shaped mountains,
multi-colored, far-vista'd, crowned heads in the sun, gigantic and inhuman, sweeping and crossing and vanishing in distance, an anarchy of perspectives, crushing and

uplifting at once, the atmosphere so pure above them that the ravens and I seem to be the only things alive in it.

I'm alone on the mountain, a mote moving in a blaze of crystal, an imperfection. An imperfection in—what? Light? Oxygen? Like the water of my fish tank, whatever fills up these spaces is effulgent but not demonstrably present, yet sometimes palpable as beaten silver. The ridges march northeast, like an alligator's back, knobbed, scarred, and green. Even the shadows are purple and cobalt. The one black is the raven's feather, drifting down, grabbed by the wind again, sailing up the green walls as though it had will and a destination. I tell the wind, *it was meant for me,* but it doesn't listen. I curl on a stone amid running water, sunning like a lizard in the golden light. *All right,* I say to the mountain, *show me something.*

I used to carry a compact duodecimo notebook with me when I went hiking. Six or seven of them still sit on my shelf, full of nonsequential notations about the forest of the state of my mind, sketches, too, some of them quite good. I was young when I began this practice, and the sophomoric profundities of some of the passages mortify me now. Nevertheless, I recognize what I was trying to do, and I recognize furthermore that I still do exactly that. I try to understand, to extract the message—for there must be a message—to me from the world. No beast but what is singing to me, no herb but what throws a shadow of magic symbols on the ground, which if I see passionately enough, I might read and understand. I have always wanted essences, distillations, quiddities. I have believed those were what I was given a mind to find. I bore my students and irritate my friends by assuming that there is a meaning to everything, and not whatever the auditor is in the mood to feel, but exactly and precisely that which the sender intended us to receive. I stained the pages of my notebook with bloodroot, drew shaky outlines of lacewings and dayflowers in order to approach a critical mass, to gather so much data that one day the world would burst open like a closet door stuffed too full. *Let me see,* was my daily prayer, and one, miraculously, almost daily answered.

You are a twelve-year-old boy. You're in love with creatures vanished from the world before the fathers of your fathers dropped from the trees. I don't mean *interested* in them; I mean in love, so night and morning pass with their lumbering mysteries of bodies yet processing, stately and unimaginable, through your dreams. You would walk out of this world without regret if the door opened on the steaming garden of former times. Your love is so great that you would abandon everything you know for a glimpse of a brachiosaur or a wooly rhino, for a look into the pool where the first amphibian was deciding not to be a fish. It is agony to you that the Veil is so permanently and, it seems, arbitrarily closed.

To address this bereavement as far as possible, you compensate with morbid attentiveness to the things which yet abound. You're there, watching, when the wake-robins bloom. You go to *another* damn museum in *another* damn city. You wait for a flitting in the underbrush to resolve into a warbler. You stop in your tracks when someone says, "Guess what I saw in the backyard yesterday." You ignore the TV programs which debunk the Loch Ness monster, not because you think there is such a thing, necessarily, but because for it to be proven not to be is another bolt driven into the ever-more-tightly-sealed door between you and the Beloved. You know you can never achieve anything really important in science because you are so driven by what you *want*. What *is* would always be taking a back seat, even if unintentionally. You turn into a crackpot, a finder-of-yeti-tracks, a filmer of lake monsters. Then you turn into a poet, where, given that delicate mixture of knowledge and passion, you can make the much-desired seem almost plausible.

The difference between a crackpot and an artist is that the artist knows that desire must be *informed*.

There will be a point when you stop describing and annotating worlds, and start creating them. That is the moment when all the joy and all the responsibility fall upon your shoulders at once, as though you really were a god. At this point it is both more and less fun, for you can't do *everything* anymore—no flying mollusks, no talking horses—but what you can do, you do with the certainty that time and a few even deals in the evolutionary poker game, and what you have imagined might really work.

How a real god could act in any other way I can't imagine.

One of my names is Dream Master. Not that I give dreams, but that I receive them, joyfully.

A dreaming man is vulnerable. The campfire dies. The moon sinks in a tangle of thorn. A bird screams once from her perch, and then the slithering coils close on her throat and she is silent. The panther pads into the circle of dying firelight. It sniffs the dreamer's hair and moves on. Perhaps it crouches in the shadows, waiting for the dreamer to wake. The quality of the dream will decide whether it attacks or purrs at the dreamer's feet. This is why there must be panthers. While the panther drowses, deciding, the dreamer is caught in a wilderness. Thick trees line both sides of the path. Something follows behind, pursuing, drawing closer and closer. The dreamer plunges ahead, hacking at the growth on all sides, waiting for the dark road to break into the open, where he can turn and fight.

Say you are a Martian scientist. The temperature of your planet under extraordinary conditions approaches the thawing point of ice. Your thin, frigid atmosphere lets stars shine through at midday, except during the stupendous red sandstorms that block out the sky for weeks, guttering out at last against the flanks of volcanoes ten miles high. Two little moons, dimmer than stars and irregular as grains of dust, wander overhead. The world is dry, cold, violent, beautiful. So it has been since Creation. This is the way worlds are.

Yet you hear queer rumors. Inexplicable complexities of metal fall onto the desert. Those who found them claimed

they whirred and clanked for a while before succumbing
to the cold. One or two insist that these things have fallen
from the sky. You find that plausible, if extreme. You aim
your instruments. In the blackness round about there is one
likely candidate, one more conceivable Home.

You send your probes to the third planet, the changeable blue world. The probes are equipped with sensors to
detect what you conceive reality to be: hard, definite, dry,
brittle, cold, red, sandy. Your expectations are low. You
prepare for failure.

Your probe lands on the roof of a house, though you
would never say exactly these words, having no concept
of "house" or anything else the little machine might meet
on Terra, but that is what has happened. The roof registers
well enough, possessing several qualities which you think
of as real. The probe bores through the flat hard dry tilted
thing into a room below. The room is full of smells, bodies and perfumes, food, sex. Bach is on the CD. The light
is greenish, dim, like a jungle thicket, which, of course, you
cannot conceive. The probe, tuned to your preconceptions,
registers "nothing." Then, with a *clink* audible to the astonished inhabitants of the "empty" room, the probe touches
the rim of a bottle of Chateau Neuf du Pape, 1963, saved
for just this evening in just this liquid season of the year.
The cork is massy and palpable, and so you cry in delight,
"There is something here!" It punctures the cork, continues down into the arterial red of the wine. But Martian
reality does not allow for nose, bouquet, the slightly stony
savor of that sunny, exquisite year, and when you break
through the bottom of the bottle, you record, "empty con-
tainer." Whoever might have been there has gone: a dead

planet, torrid, watery, too dramatic for life as it is known. In its own way, perhaps, beautiful.

～

You are God, and you have decided to make an oak. The problem is that each hillside, each river valley, demands a separate perfection. Yet you start, and in a thousand generations you have made three hundred different variations on a basic plan. Some shoot up like columns, braving the sky, daring the bolt. Some cling to the tundra, bellying along like soldiers in a trench. Some bear sweet acorns that mature in a single season, to fatten peccaries and black bears and marginal human communities, and spread a shade of round-lobed foliage over the forest floor. Some bear bitter acorns that take two years to ripen, and hurl shapes on the ground like the points of spears.

In making an oak, you see that single vision does not suffice. You loosen the bonds, break the rules, let riot prevail. Bounty gathers, overflows, becomes sheer prodigality. You take as your paradigm the whirlwind. That's not what anyone expected. Whoever looked forward to order and repose will be sorely tried. You did not plan it that way. You learned that it is what must happen.

～

You are an earless race. You shoot your probe into the hive, the nightingale's nest, the throat of the volcano. You hear nothing.

The Stirring of the Vision

CONSIDER THE PROPOSITION that certain people see things other people don't because those things wish to be seen by them.

I hike with my friend Holly in Cat Gap in the Smokies. I poke under logs for orange tiger salamanders, bright and cold enough to be molded out of vinyl. It's early spring, and every watery depression boils over with toad eggs. The eggs are appalling to the touch, like blobs out of horror movies, and of course we cannot stop ourselves from touching. At the end of the day we tally up our finds, bird, track, sign, flower, amphibian, and we are triumphant. We also realize that we have no idea where we are. Wherever we look stands another version of the same identical mountain, domed, halved, cut as abruptly by the glaciers as a baker cuts a mound of dough. As I dither, Holly points us in the right direction, triangulating by the mountains and the toad eggs and the rings of Saturn, for all I can tell. She leads us calmly home.

A literary friend and I walk a whole day in the Ohio woods. By main force we keep the topic of conversation away from books.

"Well, what did you see?" he asks at the end, fumbling for the car keys.

I tell him, "I saw white pine, wild geranium, sassafras, raccoon sign, mayapple past its prime, beech, chestnut shoots—" I cease enumerating, catching the look of flat astonishment on his face.

He says, "I saw greenish light under low leaves, how the radiance shifted from red to blue as the day went, purple now toward evening, the undersides of things paling in contrast—"

You get the point. Same woods, same day, same organs of sight, yet utter division—or complementarity—of perception.

We flatter ourselves when we put these differences down wholly to variations in human equipment and personality. Does none of the credit go to the will of the things that are seen? I don't mean to sound mystical, only true to things as I have come to perceive them. Consider:

You are an orchid. Your generations depend on your being noticed by a certain wasp that passes over your grotto once a year. They depend equally on your eluding the notice of throngs of potential orchid-munchers.

You are a gray whale. On the waves over your head fare two basic varieties of human: those who would destroy you for the riches of your body, and those who would preserve you for nearly the same reason. You cannot possibly be expected to be indifferent to this difference.

You are an April wake-robin. If your flower is picked, you will die. If your flower is picked before pollenization, the infinity of your generations dies along with you.

You are a strange, undulating creature in a cold Scottish lake. You are a hairy, wild man, like the men who rule the world, but not quite, but different enough that they will annihilate you even as they did your mutual cousins. What skill do you develop, not leaving it to chance, not leaving it to the discretion of your enemies? To disappear. When the wrong eyes are looking, simply to not be there, or if there, to be invisible.

You are a wild river. Plans for the dam are drawn, the access roads already bulldozed clear. The last scientist makes his visit. From your hidden depths you push forward a little fish, unnoticed since the beginning of the world. *Mine,* you make your rushes whisper, *mine alone. You cannot build here.*

You are a biosphere, profoundly complex, exquisitely delicate. Entering your west is an engineer loaded down with charts and measuring instruments, eyes agleam with condos and shopping complexes yet to be. Entering your east is an artist, carrying his easel over his shoulder, a poet with a dog-eared notebook in his knapsack. To whom do you show barren incommodiousness, to whom riches and bounty and mystery? It is not merely the quality of human perception which affects what is seen in the wild, or who sees it, or what quality of tongue utters it forth.

Our ineradicable sense of superiority, our need to scoff at all testimonies but our own, is the orchid's, the sea-serpent's, the yeti's, the woodland god's last weapon.

Dorothy Wordsworth, the saint and prophet of the Romantic movement, writes in her *Alfoxden Journal* on January 23, 1798:

Set forward to Stowey at half-past five. A violent storm in the wood; sheltered under the hollies. When we left home the moon immensely large, the sky scattered over with clouds. These soon closed in, contracting the dimensions of the moon without concealing her. The sound of the pattering shower, and the gusts of wind, very grand. Left the woods when nothing remained of the storm but the driving wind, and a few scattering drops of rain. Presently all clear. Venus first showing herself between the struggling clouds . . . the hawthorn hedges, black and pointed, glittering with millions of diamond drops; the hollies shining with broader patches of light. All the Heaven seemed in one perpetual motion when the rain ceased; the moon appearing, now half veiled, and now retiring behind heavy clouds, the stars still moving, the roads dirty.

Dorothy walked perpetually in the foreground of transcendent tableaux. Her brother, William's, poems, and those of their friend, Samuel Taylor Coleridge, are set with her observations like gems in an iron scabbard. Dorothy Wordsworth invents Romanticism for the English mind, centering on the conviction that nature has a message for us if we but look, will transfigure us if we but open and drink it in. Most artists are blind beside her. Why did she *see* so surpassingly and unforgettably? The expected answer is that she was profoundly alert, receptive to the point of, and eventually past the point of, madness.

The *true* answer is that she was chosen.

The deer is an animal with which I have no rapport. I know you are meant to sit in some likely spot and wait patiently

for them to come to you, but life is short. So I crunch on
through the undergrowth, singing, chattering aloud, an-
swering the woodpeckers, and the damn skittish quad-
rupeds can approach or stay away, as it pleases them. I
would starve were I an American Indian or a pioneer.
The first time I ever saw a wild deer was when my father's
Rambler station wagon was crashing into one on a
Pennsylvania road, as we went over the river and through
the woods to grandmother's house for Thanksgiving. I
could see its muzzle and red left eye just as it failed to
clear the front of the car in a mighty leap from the roadside,
just as the rest of its body was sagging the grill and radiator
like wet cardboard. The deer died after brief throes, which
I watched, hoping that the movements were the struggles
of the buck to rise, which would presently be answered by
success. It was not to be. The whole episode seemed too
odd to me, a murderous collision of two powers which, if
the world were right, would never meet at all. Deer hair
clogged the broken grill, somehow sucked in, to bristle
from the sticky engine and whirl about pipes and wires.
It was as though deer and Rambler had tried to consume
each other.

Still, I do see deer, live ones, and am always grateful.
Easing down the northeast slope of Young Pisgah, I hear
hoof-falls, see the white flags of nervous does. They are
not really very afraid of me, but lope off like mediocre ac-
tors following their blocking. They are so disinclined to
be really afraid that I allow myself to hope that if I creep
with only moderately increased caution from one thicket
to another I might actually see one up close. Even as I think
this, it happens, and as the hunters' wisdom suggests, it is
the deer that come to me. I hear something moving

through the brush, quite near. I stop dead. She has entered a grove of laurel, high over the parkway, thirty feet away. She looks down the road as though waiting for some specific vehicle to pass, not skittish, as I expected, but merely cautious. Her pelt is very dark, not "fawn" at all, but gray and dark steel.

I sense the instant when she senses me. Her white tail flies up, then down, unsure yet what my intentions are, unsure whether I see her, and therefore whether it would be better for her to count on invisibility, or to run. Luck puts me downwind. Staring straight at me, she stamps a forehoof, trying to startle me into giving myself away. She does this several times, making her hoof pause in midair before bringing it down with a sharp, ringing sound. As she stamps, the expression in her eyes changes, from mere alertness to something resembling cunning, as though with each stamp saying aloud, *Now I have you, ape.* But she doesn't have me. I stand still as a stump. I'm not going to be the one to ruin the moment.

Then she does an amazing thing. She begins to walk toward me, deliberately, casually, hoof after hoof. I scarcely dare to breathe. When half the distance between us is gone, she turns and, with no gesture of fear, strolls back to her grove of laurel, defecates, prances high and mighty back down the mountain, neither hurrying nor lagging, indifferent as a goddess. The trail makes a switchback, dropping several times beneath the lip over which I had frightened the other deer. I walk to the rim and see the deer tribe arrayed beneath me like a diorama of The Wilderness. I feel the descent of grace abundant.

I walk on down to Bent Creek, returning twice as fast as I had come. I watch the sun set behind Laurel Mountain,

descending Young Pisgah in a flood of twilight pastels
which to tell of were to diminish—flamingo and peony,
turquoise and cerulean and cobalt and bluebird, gray
and silver and dove, all slashed with the royal velvet of
the shadows of the trees. At such an hour you fear to
touch anything, not a tree nor a rose-cane glowing in
their unnatural lavender, not a leaf, fearing they are
phantoms, fearing they will not really be there to receive
the touch. In the deep valley an owl calls, unfurling his
quiet wing.

～

A masterpiece of seventeenth century prose is Nicholas
Culpeper's *Complete Herbal.* It is a scientific text, as that
term was understood in 1640, and carefully distinguishes
between those things that are "known" and those merely
purported by the ignorant or hopeful. Culpeper never
spares technical vocabulary for the sake of a popular tone,
and he harrumphingly assumes a high level of awareness
in his readership, as when he speaks of the broom plant:
"To spend time in writing a description hereof is altogether
needless, it being so generally used by all the good housewives almost throughout the land to sweep their houses
with." Good sense, good health, a modern perspective
pervade all.

If you look up "goldenrod" in the *Herbal,* you will
find a usable description of the plant, its habitat and
blooming time, with the added benefit that Culpeper's
botanic descriptions read like Marianne Moore poems.
After the description of goldenrod comes a section called
"Government and Virtues." Here Culpeper writes:

Venus rules this herb. It is a balsamic, vulnerary herb, long famous against inward hurts and bruises. . . . Few things exceed it in the gravel, stones in the reins and kidneys, strangury, and where are small stones so situated as to cause heat and soreness. . . . It is a sovreign wound-herb, inferior to none, both for inward and outward use. It is good to stay the immoderate flux of women's courses, the bloody flux, ulcers, and in lotions to wash the privy parts in venereal cases.

Quaint, yes, but we do Culpeper an injustice to assume he is naive. His science is as correct and modern as it could be made. It adheres to his sense of reality with elegance and completeness. Nothing is untidy, nothing left over or cut against the grain. Culpeper is not only a botanist and physician, but also (and almost necessarily at the time) an astrologer, who knew by reason and observation that the fate of men is tied to the great dance of the stars, who read the signatures of the planets in the wayside herbs. It is all a beautiful unity to him. It is no more superstitious—which is to say, no more or less demonstrable— than modern physics. To the "vulgar" unacquainted with astrology he writes,

Kind souls, I am sorry it hath been your sad mishap to have been so long trained in such Egyptian darkness, even darkness which to your sorrow may be felt. The vulgar road of physic is not in my practice, and I am therefore the more unfit to give you advice.

Those who want mere *medicine*, mere *chemistry*, can just go look somewhere else. Culpeper was not only one of the last men of astrology (magic died a long death; remember that Isaac Newton cast horoscopes and tried to alchemize base metals) but also one of the first of science. After enumerating the received properties of the ash tree, he adds,

> I can justly except against none of this, save only the first, *viz*—that ash tree tops and leaves are good against the biting of serpents. I suppose this had its rise from Gerard or Pliny, both which hold that there is such an antipathy between the adder and an ash-tree, that if an adder be encompassed around with ash-tree leaves, she would sooner run through fire than through the leaves; the contrary to which is truth, as both my eyes are witness.

Imagine the experiment—which, in any case, was obviously *done*. Culpeper knew the difference between vulgar supposition and provable truth.

Yet for all his being right-minded, his conclusions were wrong. Why? That it was so is not a matter of perception—for his perception was flawless—but of aesthetics. Men of old missed the big bang and natural selection less because of ignorance than because of the beauty of the alternatives. How *beautiful* that the mark of Venus should be graven on the goldenrod. How *beautiful* that the stars hang in crystal spheres ply over ply above Foundation Earth—so beautiful that it almost doesn't matter whether it is *actual* or not.

When do perceptions change and enlarge?

When the mind changes and enlarges the set of things that it calls beautiful.

Johannes Kepler could not let loose of his Perfect Shapes until he saw the beauty of the ellipse. The religious establishment could not (cannot, I should say, in some cases) embrace evolution until it perceived the superior splendor of everlasting labor over instantaneous will. Progress is made in science when someone, a Darwin, an Einstein, finds the next step unavoidably seductive.

Advances in knowledge are advances in aesthetics.

Beauty propels the sciences when the sciences are true.

Learning is seduction. We learn the secrets of the mountain and the rainbow when we begin to desire them. We change cosmologies when a lovelier one appears. If we long for it desperately enough, elegant experiments appear to prove the "rightness" of it—which will, of course, seem laughable at the next convulsion of desire.

All as it should be. Beauty is truth; truth, beauty. Remember that one?

 Why do I see the heron and the woodpecker and the orange salamander when I go into the forest? Because they are beautiful to me. I desire them, and love, far from being blind, has hawk's eyes. Here is the creepier part, but I will say it anyway: I see them because they know of my love and desire, and they come to me. Vision validates what is seen. All creation, therefore, longs to be seen. To be loved, go through the world with your eyes open.

New worlds debut not from prophecies but from the mating of loud birds on a branch, a doe striking her fore-foot on the ground, the twisted shadow of a heron passing over the moon, a pattern hitherto unsuspected, a beauty so unprepared for, it must either be rejected, or convulse the soul.

Friends take me caving. I've never been before, and though I'm not claustrophobic, close places do not exactly delight me. I'm frightened, actually, but I know I fear the idea of *descending* rather than the cave itself. When I arrive at the cave mouth, I am neither apprehensive nor excited, but calm, possessing the absurd yet inescapable conviction that I have been there before.

We enter the cave from the north. There are two sounds. Water is one, flowing water, both above us, in the world of light, and below us in the world of mystery. I listen for a long time before recognizing that the other one is the drone of bees. The bees have burrowed in from outside and have laid their honey down in living rock. If you let your consciousness go for a second, their sound merges with the sound of the water and the half-palpable reverberation of the cave to make one sound, an uttered syllable, invariable and eternal.

Beyond the reach of our flashlights I expect black. It is, however, purple. We aim the lamps outward, pretending to look for blocks or passages, but really looking at the purple, pushing it back to where it is deepest, walking into the midst of it, feeling it close around us, purple that makes us realize we have never seen that color before. Beside this, every other shade of it is smoky or watery. This is True Purple, a midnight jewel, the mother of porphyry, a dark fire that lives without consuming. My friend, remembering my earlier nervousness, asks me how I feel. I answer, "Fine"; what I mean is, *Welcome.*

At what seems to be the bottom of the cave lies a clear pool. I dip my hand in. Under the water, my hand takes on the color of stone, pale, clean, animate, impervious, a living crystal. At this moment I am most frightened, and most at home.

Summer

I'M JOGGING PISGAH HIGHWAY, between the trailers and the narrow farms whose back acres begin to climb the mountains. They're not used to people running this road. Jogging is suburban, leisurely. This is not suburbia, and leisure is spent with guns and beer. Here, if you run, you have something behind you, a bear, or a husband home too soon. The men feel naked without their dusty pickups, their well-loved, third-hand Chevies. Almost naked by any standard, I dismay and bewilder them. They want to close the drapes on me. They want me safe inside, for my sake and for theirs. My neighbors pass, waving uncertainly through their windshields, unsure whether, me running in the heat of the day with no reason and all, everything is all right. I wave back to let them know it's all right, to assure them I am harmless.

An onlooker would not know this, but I am going long and steady today for a particular reason. It is because I run through successive curtains of perfume. I am breathing as hard as I can breathe, and it is not from the running. Wild rose. Ditch water. Carrion. Wild rose. Cow. Wild rose. Wild rose. Under everything: honeysuckle, pervasive as a weed in these parts. The scent of the road is dust, ambrosia, attar, carrion—sickly to the sickly, to the ravished, ravishing.

When I pause my own scent comes about me like a cloud. This is what my lovers, what the beasts of the forest know of me, a smell of dust and sweat and sun-struck body. Ambrosial. I like it. I think I am generally too clean.

The roadside perfumes flow in like water as I breathe. As with all drowning, the secret is to lie back. Dream. Open every opening you have to open. Take it in.

I pluck on the run a honeysuckle flower from vines overhanging the ditches. It is gold and pale, a sweet entanglement walling the low banks, veiling opossum corpses, veiling puddles rainbowed with the oils of wrecks. I bite the base for a moment's nectar, for that day-hot droplet, the spurt of an elfin lover, the last drink in a desert made of green. It bursts in my mouth like sun and honey. Like Titan Hummingbird, I take fire and run.

The perfume lures me by the least gesture of its hand. It takes me by the whisper of a touch. My neighbor sees me slowing, but he guesses the reason wrong. Tired, he supposes. He gestures, "Want a ride?" I wave him on. I am not coming home just now. I may not ever, depending on how long the road will let me.

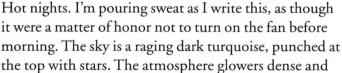

Hot nights. I'm pouring sweat as I write this, as though it were a matter of honor not to turn on the fan before morning. The sky is a raging dark turquoise, punched at the top with stars. The atmosphere glowers dense and close. It's not unpleasant, but rather as though one lived at the bottom of a chasm with air heaped in sweet, crushing layers above. It is a pure heat, made new after yesterday's thunderstorms, that came in colossal animal-shaped clouds, rolling in gold fire from the west.

I drive to Craggy Dome to climb. I pretend to climb to escape the heat; if that had actually been my intention, it would have worked. I pull my jacket around my shoulders, savoring the exotic feeling of a summer chill.

If you come to Craggy Dome in winter, you'll hear ravens cackling to themselves in midair, like sorcerers just that moment transformed, still carrying on old gossip in their hard new voices. I come here when I'm sad. Sheer spectacle takes the mind off itself. Spectacle is why God gets away with so much, why He dares to leave our deepest questions unanswered. We ask, why is there suffering? Why is there death? And He answers with whirlwinds and quasars and breaching leviathans. Our breath's taken away. We can't put the question a second time.

Mist whirls up from the valley, curls over the crag like a veil, before plunging down again, studded with fluttering swallows. It is for the swallows a fortunate turbulence, carrying them up and down a thousand feet of rock, they needing only to keep their beaks open for the bugs to fly in. The mountain stands before me, and I before the mountain.

I lie reading in bed after a scorching day, cool with the aftermath of a shower, with an hour of lying still. I hear a sound, a rush, a roaring, that could be taken for a great wave breaking. I look out my window to see if a water pipe has burst or a tank truck sprung a leak. I walk to the opposite window to check the neighboring parking lot, and as I watch, rain appears at the top of the light and plunges with perceptible slowness to the ground. That was the cause of the roaring, though the sound preceded the visible rain by half a minute, as though it first struck the crowns of trees a thousand feet high.

A cardinal pipes hysterically in the willow outside my study window. I scan the ground for the cat or the fallen chick which might be disturbing her. Nothing. Perhaps the attack is from Above. Perhaps she is scolding God for keeping the rain so long, then sending it with so much noise.

~

Tourists were feeding the bears. They stayed in their cars, mostly, as the signs warned them to do, and the black bears, mostly females with young, politely waited for the food to be dropped on the ground. There were a few ruined paint jobs from the scraping of claws, maybe, but many would think that a small price to pay to be so near a wild animal.

The cubs bawled when they thought they weren't getting enough: bread, Fritos, chips, Twinkies, pretzels, one idiot pouring beer into his hand, then letting it drip on their upturned muzzles.

I parked a way off from the bear feeding station, wanting to hike, but not wanting to deal with either tourists or bears. I had a backpack of the colors of the American flag then, red, white, and blue in shiny material like vinyl, but supple and warm to the touch, that my sister had bought for me during the Bicentennial. This story is partially to tell her what happened, why she never saw me use it. That day I used it, hoisting it on my back and scrurrying into the woods in high summer, when the anemones and bloodroots were green ghosts fading into green shadows.

Fifty paces from the road I encountered an old bear sow. I saw no cub, but her teats were swollen. Perhaps she cuffed her baby up a tree when she saw me coming. I was not happy with the situation. For a bear, people in cars on the road are natural, expectable, not a threat. A lone human in the forest is another thing altogether, much more threatening, or, I feared she might think, much more of an opportunity. The bear's posture broadcast indecision. She shook her head slowly, an indication of anxiety that I figured she'd get over if I neither hesitated nor increased my pace. She'd see I was no threat. I intended to pass calmly by, turning neither right nor left. It was for moments like this that I had mastered—so I thought—the ways of the forest.

I wasn't especially afraid even when she came close, even when she reared back on her hind legs in a gesture that may have been meant as a threat, but that coming from her seemed comic and ungainly. I turned my back on her and continued into the forest. She was very quiet, and I didn't hear her moving, quite quickly, as it turned out, over the leaf litter.

My neck snapped backward in a stationary whiplash when she bit into my American flag backpack, pushing my body violently forward with her paws to separate it from me. It worked. I felt the shoulder straps rip, then the sudden cool of air on my back. I knew enough not to run, nor, God knows, to whirl around and try to get the backpack back. Instead, I stood and watched. Not angry, not afraid, merely astonished.

A few rips told her there was nothing edible in the backpack. She backed up a few paces in order to look up into
my face. She, as I, was curious. What was I doing carrying
something that you couldn't eat? The ways of these humans
were inexplicable. We stared at each other for a long moment. Noise was coming from the road. She turned her
head to face it, and that broke the spell. In a moment she
was wandering off, a long piece of my patriotic backpack
hanging from her muzzle. I think she had forgotten that
I existed. When the shock of the exchange was over, I
looked down and noted that my left pant leg was gone,
and that her claw had left a gash eight inches long down
the back of my leg. She had meant nothing by it. She used
my leg to steady herself as she would have the limb of a
tree, and with the same consequence.

~~~

*Rumors fly. Voices whisper that the world may not be as we
believed. It may be more beautiful, more dangerous, more
fragile, more foreign. We resist, for to change world view is
to change ourselves, and for that we are not ready. Denial is
a powerful force, and we can deny for a long time before the
voices start again. Someone suggests that truth is better than
comfort. We try to agree. We burn the old scriptures; we march
in the streets; we turn against the superstitions of our fathers.
Still, we don't see everything we feel must be there to be seen.
We ask,* How shall we come to know?

*Someone answers that we must put on new eyes. We must
see the world as at the first, preconceptions cut away, and along
with preconceptions, safety. We must be as children exiled from*

our fathers' houses, abandoned to the Greenwood, left to find the way by scattering crumbs behind us.

It is too hard! *we say, trying to turn back. But our fathers' houses are already gone. The tulip saplings already have burst through the roofs. Sparrows hop from one foot to the other, waiting for the next crumb. They have swallowed them all. There is no way back.*

~~~

When I was a kid in Akron I had a room with windows on the north and west. Summer nights, I left them open so the wind blew through, toppling knickknacks from the dresser, switching the hems of the curtains against the wall. Wind carried the scent of Eastwood marsh and the noise of the farm boys roaring in from Hartville on a Saturday night. Factory smoke from the city lying westward dimmed the stars, but I didn't know it could be otherwise, and believed the heavens were everywhere as I saw them, misty, dichrome ink and pale until the moon rose in Halloween orange.

I'd hear my little black and white dog barking; I'd run to the window. Usually it was just the moon: maddening canine vigilance with an immaterial invasion, a moon too huge for a boy to cover with this hand even if he spreads his fingers wide. Sometimes, though, it was a solitary runner. Dressed in white, he held his arms close at his sides as though wanting to take up as little space as possible. I guess he lived in the housing project where it flooded in spring and all the houses were made of pastel aluminum. That was the direction he'd run from, padding almost silent

to the southeast. Of course, he could have been from anywhere. He could have run from Greece with the Olympic
torch still smouldering in a bus station locker. A few dogs,
like mine, relieved the watches of the night with a moment's barking and a lunge at his shoes. He didn't seem
upset, didn't break stride. After our patch of houses, he
ran alone.

I thought about what he might do once he got to the
park, I thought about what he would do running alone in
the woods. The stories say there are Ladies there, made of
moonlight, their white hair shivering in the wind. There
are creatures there, driven inward and condensed by the
growing city long ago. Abandoned gods, derelict souls,
phantoms dreaming in the dark until the sound of his
shoes, the rainy swish of his shorts against his singlet, came
to wake them.

People stopped seeing the runner when I was away
at school. Nobody took his place. I decided once that I
would, though the route has changed, and the profound
dark of the Eastwood marsh is lit on one side by a Kmart.
I pull on my running shoes, going over in my mind what
must have been the solitary runner's route. I trot by my
own window, as he always did. I assume someone is staring at me through the parted curtains. I hold my arms
tight at my sides. I turn my face from the blare of the
Kmart, canceling its existence with my disregard. *Dogs!*
I yell into back yards, if I've run too far unnoticed.

At the Route 91 intersection, it's a point of honor
not to stop. You leap across the pavement, far enough from
the cars for safety, near enough for effect. A horn or the
screeching of brakes is the sign of insufficient elegance.

Closeness is perfection, the hissing intake of breath from the driver's seat, the brake foot hovering midair.

Eastwood Road is still dark, unlighted. The bare fields on either side are scoured by the tracks of dirt bikes. The blue hulk of the forest looms on the south side. The ground isn't level, but not so tilted as to slow me down. I cover myself from the oncoming headlights, less against the glare than so as not to be recognized in my hometown, not to have my name shouted in the night air and the spell be broken. I am not who I was. I am the midnight runner.

Times have changed. Neighborhoods have crept closer; there are more windows to try not to glance into; there are girls in pairs and gaggles braving the long bare of the road in their shorts and T-shirts. Two of these girls have convinced the drive-through liquor store clerk that they are of age. This can be done if you're on foot. The clerks are used to handing bottles and change through car windows, and a full-front person puts them off stride. The girls have in their brown bag, I bet, amaretto, to sip in their rooms or to pour into cola and drink wickedly in the living room in front of their parents. They think themselves bold to be here at twilight, almost alone. Beyond the drive-through liquor store, the city fails, no business, no houses until Morningview Drive, just the long black flank of the city park.

The girls see me. They lean together to whisper. They waver, turn back toward the liquor store. They don't want to be caught between patches of civilization with a strange man loping in white gym shorts. The pimply clerk will think that they have turned back for him.

I try to smile as we pass. My anxiety for the smile not to be a leer probably makes it one. Whatever expression I am wearing doesn't feel right on my face. My knees hurt on the uneven ground. I forget my face and concentrate on that. I have been spending too much energy on the girls. Nothing will come of that. They keep walking, arms stiff at sides, eyes forward in an expression meant to convey indifference, but which actually conveys dread and curiosity. Maybe I'm enjoying this. The footpath beside the road is six feet wide, but they huddle together, shoulder to shoulder. I hear the dark one say to the tall one, "Don't tell mother!"

I turn onto the park road. It lies bright under the moon. I feel the girls watching me, safe now that my back is turned, their scrutiny like a breeze on the back of my neck. What? What weren't they going to tell mother? Probably about the liquor, but I hope about me.

The park curves by a huge water tower that sings if you touch it. I learned this from a boy who was my friend because his father and mine were friends. I didn't like him so much. He was always telling me things about radios and electricity and engines, things in which I had no interest. But he showed me how to hit the tower, high up, with a stick or a stone, and it will go, *Ba-huuuuuuuuummmm-mmm.* It was wonderful, really, like a deep-voiced oracle in the middle of the bikers' field.

The weeds of the north meadow march steel-colored in the darkness. Hardhack, goldenrod, Joe-pye, queen-of-the-meadow, hawkweed, wild rose in its murderous tangle, a smell there like tea steeped all day in a copper kettle. Every hawkweed sprouts from a place where a hawk has made a kill, so a camp counselor told us long ago, I think that in all the history of the world, there should have been more hawks. I am dismayed that in all the history of hawks, every single spot of ground should not, by now, have enjoyed the honor of a kill. I pass tiny runways of life, mouse runs, rabbit forms, man tracks, lit by the shimmer of the flat sky. The blind must feel this way, running by feel, by dead reckoning, by luck. I cross from the open field into the forest.

Utterly blind at first, I know the path from memory, and navigate after a minute by the faint purple radiance of the forest floor. The way is a ribbon of the dimmest conceivable light, but enough, but plenty. Anything could be watching from the underbrush, and I wouldn't know. But I hope for the worst. I watch for man shape or beast shape rearing in the shadows. I know I could handle it. I know it would probably mean me well.

I used to be able to sicken myself with fantasies of monsters, but that was before I had known anything really terrible. Like the Japanese urchin crooning his love-song to Godzilla, I longed for night's worst children a fraction more than I dreaded them.

Running hard now, confident of footing. I must be bright in this black, a flame, a phantom, with my white shorts and white skin. The night things hesitate toward me, curious but uncertain. I'm the one to watch, the ambiguous apparition loping in the dark, swearing at the occasional slick spot or twisted root. Sweat cools on my chest. I quicken my pace to keep warm.

The path loops into the pines. Fewer bugs, the fragrance that I'd know was *earth* if I smelled it lost in the stars for a thousand years. A sudden blue opens before me. It is the great south meadow of the park, newly mown, knife-edged, choking with perfumes. The field is bound on the south by Newton Street, which I can reach now in a three-minute sprint. I jump into the field, bounding like an animal, to show it I am there. I scan underfoot to find the footprints of the solitary runner, in whose steps I run, for proof that this is the right way. I don't have to make it to Newton Street tonight; there is no reason to go to the limit, to do it all right now. I turn back, homeward, picking up speed, pine, oak, scrub, meadow, toward the Singing Tower. I'm going as fast as I dare, the uneven land rocking my feet left and right. Westward, clouds tear, and the young moon snags on the crowns of tulips.

Out on the road, the girls are long gone. Speed, speed, all downhill now. I whoop at the chained dogs. I watch windows for curtains parting, for the eyes of the sleepless looking out at me.

$$\approx$$

Climbing the hill to do my laundry, I found an ovenbird. It was sitting on the cement walk. I picked her up, gently, seeing no wound that could explain her docility. I cradled her in my hands, amazed, as one always is, by her smallness, her weightlessness, at her beauty, the greenish-gold-brown of her back, the electric streaks of dark across her blinding white breast, the subtle crown of sun's orange, scarcely more than a shimmer of light. She regarded me with black, untroubled eyes. It was a blessing to hold her, but a blessing weighted somehow with *wrong*. What was

amiss that she should let me get so close, that she should
endure my hand, that she should almost nestle. I set her
on the fence rail and went in to do the wash. In the laundry room sat another ovenbird—her mate, I supposed—
trapped and disoriented in the complicated room. I herded
him through the door. They met, chirped briefly, fluttered
off into the trees.

I know what I am supposed to think.

Also what I *do* think.

I've spent another month in Ireland, my favorite place in
the world, and the plane touches down at the Asheville
airport. I am trying not to be sad. It is July. July in Ireland
can be bracingly cold, torn with rainstorms, chilled by
great winds off the Atlantic, lit by an atmosphere of such
spare brightness that it seems there is less of it than there
is here, which even in storm gleams with a diamond clarity. Furthermore, Ireland is so far north that there are days
in my journey when I never see darkness, but go to bed in
the lingering twilight, rise up in the blaze of morning. But
now I am back, on a continent, a big one, far inland. I step
out onto the tarmac, and what I feel is heat, voluptuous,
damp, pervading, heat radiating from a sky many layers
thicker than the one I have grown used to. And what is
more, it is dark, really, really *dark*. My ride whisks me away
into a midnight jungle of rich textures and rich smells, vibrant with the beating of insect wings. I set my luggage
down in my own house, turn off the lights, just planted
there in the close dark, sweating, smiling, feeling hot and

moist and sexy, and there are bugs to be swatted, and the vines are tearing at the window screens, and the moon is a great swollen blue oyster, and everything is rich and dark and sweating and big, and it is summer, and I am *home*.

Professions

FOR A WHILE I EARNED my living as the sort of naturalist who leads people through the forest, telling them what flutters, scurries, burrows, photosynthesizes around them. The grand name for this is "interpretive naturalist," though my term for it at the time was "scrambling for a job." At the level where I functioned, lack of official training did not seem to be a detriment. To obtain the position one took a civil service exam on which one was asked questions like, "Would you put vertical stripes or bright-colored blotches on the costume of an actor to make him look taller?" I knew the answer to that, so I was accepted by the parks department. I could tell a tortoise from a mad dog, so I was assigned to Nature Day Camp. The Akron, Ohio, Parks and Recreation Department could have done a lot worse actually. I wanted the job. I am morbidly conscientious. I knew what I was doing. The only odd thing, really, is that I couldn't have explained *why* I knew what I was doing. I just did. Maybe the following pages will provide a sort of an explanation.

Parks & Rec hauled urban and suburban kids to my park in a bus driven by a handsome Latino named Lou. Lou wore a heavy gold chain and a medallion bright as the moon in the black hair of his chest. I admired what I took to be the Mediterranean emancipation of his body, foreign to the T-shirted and vehemently underweared Protestantism I had known all my life.

Lou's expression when he pulled up told me how the day was going to be. If he laughed and joked, it would be an easy day filled with well-behaved and parentally admonished kids, grateful for an outing. If Lou arrived scowling— well, to adapt Tolstoy's maxim concerning families, good days were just good days, while every disaster dwells in memory with appalling uniqueness.

Among the players was David, a fourteen-year-old neighborhood kid who buzzed us with his dirt bike, until one day I offered him half of my sandwich, after which he couldn't be pried from my side until quitting time, displaying a devotion that, though quieter than the dirt bike, was scarcely less wearing. Few have adored me since with quite the same single-mindedness, even ferocity, and I wish I had appreciated it at the time.

There too was Margaret, my co-worker, placed there by some perverse levity of bureaucracy. Margaret hated the outdoors. She wore nylons to hike in. She summoned me to slay any flying thing that came near her that was not demonstrably a bird or a butterfly. She presided over lunch time like a Dickensian orphanage-keeper, hoarding the sandwiches until exactly the right moment, doling out the extras according to a scale of deservedness fathomed only by herself.

Sometimes our charges were suburban kids—mall rats at just the time when the species was coming into being—who exhausted themselves with the effort to appear uninterested. Nothing could be done for them. Send them back to the mall and set it down as a day wasted.

Sometimes they were ghetto kids who were not used to wildlife that was neither roach nor dog. Every sound terrified them. Every waving branch stopped them dead in their tracks, waiting for instruction, waiting for protection. I could allay some of their fears by asking, "What's the worst thing you could meet up with in the woods?" and when they went through the possibilities, even when they included bears and Dracula, they understood that they themselves were the most fearsome beings in the valley. This was in the early seventies, before you could find a crack pipe under every picnic table.

Our rounds through the forest included chestnut sprouts rising from stumps stricken when their grandfathers were boys. I made them wade in the Cuyahoga— miles above where it took fire in the Flats of Cleveland—to make them feel living waters at their knees, to see kingfishers zoom to their dinners at eye level, and eight-pound carp, dreadnought in the deep water midstream, grown to dull gold leviathans after having been flushed from the garden pools of Cuyahoga Falls and down the plumbing of Akron. I held out the long muscle of the garter snake, to let the boldest of them touch.

I'd never seen such frightened people before. Green made them uneasy. The flutter of a leaf or the chattering of a squirrel edged them toward panic. They feared open spaces as the deer do. When I brought them to the river to wade, they huddled on the shore, touching their toes gingerly to the surface, holding themselves and shivering. Anything I told them about the world was news.

See here? The miter of jack-in-the-pulpit, the seed pod phallic and provocative in the green of high summer. There, spiderwort, cool blue on a day that blazes with heat already through the tree tops. I want to pluck the flower and gobble it down, still covered with morning dew. I confess this to my charges and they say, *Eeeewwww.*

That? The wallop of the pileated woodpecker, crow-sized, fire-headed, jack-hammering mad woman of the woods, cousin to the ghostly ivory-billed, who, like Arthur and Elijah, is much-rumored, but returns finally only at the end of time.

I lead them down a path cut for a power line. The path connects the river with the power station downtown, a distance of two miles. Hollyhock and wild raspberry bloom on all sides, droning with bees. Sweet pea kisses our ankles as we walk. I don't tell them that in the morning, before the buses arrive, this is the dormitory of the bums, asleep, most of them, hungover and sleeping it off, but once in a while, flat out dead. To tell the dead ones from the drunk ones you must touch. Kick and yell if, after the touch, you are still uncertain.

I pluck a leaf off a shiny, oily-green vine, hold it aloft, and say, "Does anybody know what *this* is?" When the answer, poison ivy, is finally revealed, I wait for the squeal, "But you're holding it in your *hand!*" I don't know if I'm immune or not, but I must be, for time after time the stunt works to gratifying result.

A tame—though still wild—raccoon put in a dramatic appearance when it suited his ends, these ends being scraps of lunch. If we passed in the morning, he ignored us. If we passed in the afternoon, he launched into his act, knowing somehow that Margaret had doled out the sandwiches and dry apples, that many of the children had kept uneaten against just such an event. The bolder children could touch him if they dared, but only on the paws, and only in the act of handing him food. In some ways it was irresponsible to allow contact with a wild raccoon, a powerful and unpredictable animal, but I saw as one of my major tasks to get children comfortable with nature. Flapping "friendly" animals away with my T-shirt sent the wrong message. My teenage friend David called the raccoon "Debbie," though it was certainly a wily old boar.

The role of Mr. Debbie in our afternoon walks changed abruptly one day when we were accompanied by a large dog, a yellow shepherd-and-something mix. The dog too was taken in by the raccoon's placid demeanor, and attacked it as the children watched. Debbie rolled over on his back, caught the mongrel's throat in his teeth, held it tight over his own supine body, raking his claws through the astonished dog's flesh, in a few seconds disemboweling it before the children's transfixed but oddly unhorrified eyes. When Debbie released it, the dog scrambled to its feet, with its guts trailing on the ground, whimpering a little until it sagged to the ground from blood loss. It was dead in five minutes. The children were very quiet. Not one of them mentioned the incident to Lou as they climbed back onto the bus. He noticed their gravity and absorption, and shrugged at me a little thanks for a quiet ride home.

That night I received a phone call from one furious

parent. His son could not sleep. Furthermore, he believed I had staged the entire incident.

～

I taught for a year at Hiram College, in Ohio, my alma mater. It was a good year, a fulfillment of certain of life's currents and the initiation of others. I knew that whatever came after must be so different from what had come before that no bridge would span the gap. A clean break, stinging and medicinal, would be necessary.

Because of this feeling of transition—and, it must be said, out of concern for space in the moving van—I took boxes of letters saved through the years and threw them into the dumpster behind my apartment building. Old lovers, family, friends, teachers, adversaries mingled with beer cans and onion peels. It was a grievous and desperate thing to do, but I've never regretted it—maybe because of what happened in the dark of that night.

The U-Haul was fully loaded, nonessentials sold or given away. I lay for the last time in my apartment, in a sleeping bag on the floor, not sleeping. Excitement and anxiety kept me tossing, until a disturbance in the backyard badgered me fully to my feet. In the light of the parking lot lamp, I saw a family of raccoons rooting through the dumpster, bright eyes ablaze, droll and grave by turns, pawing through the remnants of the day. One had a sheet in its mouth that I recognized, the dark ink on blue paper of someone who had once meant something to me. The letter had been very, very sad. The letter in the clown mouth of the baby 'coon was very, very funny.

A transfiguration. A redemption. What the raccoons made of my letters I can't say, but it delighted me to think of them there, mingling with my life in so direct and physical a way. I hoped they would eat, consume, digest, take the fragments of my lost life with them, so they might not be so utterly come to an end.

∼

"Naturalist" was the most satisfying job I had as a youth, and when I ask myself why I gave it up, I realize it has something to do with *propriety,* the eventual coming to the rightness of one's life through a blizzard of possibilities. Another way of saying that is to observe that one's love may be genuine, but the expression nevertheless inappropriate. I am a writer. It is right that I am a writer. I grew up almost sure to be a scientist.

What kind of scientist I was sure to be changed from year to year. After reading Roy Chapman Andrews, I loved dinosaurs with fierce love. I was jealous and obsessive. Another boy's playing with my plastic pterosaurs drove me wild. The nightmare wings belonged in my hands alone. Typical of any first passion, I have never completely recovered. To this day, though I'd cross the street to see the Pope or the Mona Lisa, I'd crawl on hands and knees through bog and glacial moraine for a really hideous fossil.

When I read a boy's book of great archaeological discoveries—Carter in Egypt, Schliemann at Troy, Evans at Knossos—I peopled my thoughts with divine kings and golden empires.

The dinosaurs and the lost civilizations had in common

pastness, the possibility that what we know of them is the least that can be known, that they were much huger, fiercer, grander, richer than the fragmentary record allows us to assert. The space between the remnants and the possibility could be filled up with the imagination.

It was not quite the same thing when someone bought me a Golden Book of the solar system, over which I pored in the first grade to the detriment of other studies. Here was something so immense that even sober scientific understatement bristled with millions of light years, billions of years, thousands of degrees Kelvin. Science class was my favorite because everything was so *vivid.* Subjects screamed, flew, expired in fire, exploded, hurled through the frozen void—I was seeking poetry, but couldn't know it so long as the poetry I knew had to do with witches on switches and fairies in the garden. I have always loathed the pretty. Poetry then was pretty; science wasn't.

The first mentionable money I had was ten dollars from some ancestor or other. My parents insisted on banking half "for college"—the sweet naivete of that strikes me only now—but the rest I had for myself. I knew what I wanted as soon as it was in my hands. I dragged my parents to the five-and-dime to buy me five Golden Book nature guides, which one could get for a buck apiece back then: *Birds, Mammals, Reptiles and Amphibians, Insects, The Seashore. The Seashore* was boring (maybe because I had never seen one), but the others I read, reread, memorized, learned so well that any lecture by a teacher was bound to be a rehash and a disappointment. I corrected my teachers. I failed to pay attention, because I already knew more than she who was speaking. I became a behavioral problem of minor proportions, all because of my Golden Books of nature.

My friend Ronnie got a chemistry set for Christmas. We spent the vacation as mad scientists, mixing unspeakable brews, creating lingering stinks, all in the name of advancing science. I saved my pennies and bought a gas-blue volume called *The Human Body*, where I learned words like "endocrine," "testicle," "medulla oblongata," which temporarily raised hope in my mother that I might become a doctor.

Yet it wasn't actually the science that interested me. I wouldn't have had the vocabulary to express it, but the fascination was aesthetic rather than scientific. I acted like a scientist because it was a nifty thing to do. It was drama. In a time when boys weren't sent to dance class or given piano lessons or encouraged to draw anything but cars and cowboys, in the era of *Sputnik,* when art was de-emphasized for the sake of science, it was practically the one acceptable expression of the aesthetic impulse. I wanted theater. The role I played was scientist because it was, so far as I could tell, the lead.

I could have continued to play the scientist. I wouldn't have been a very good one, though with my stunned appreciation of scientific discoveries, I might have been a useful science teacher. Eventually, circumstance showed me a more direct route to the desire of my heart. For me, science was a doorstep into art. For some, the sequence is reversed. However it works, the impulses of science and the impulses of art are at first indivisible, a single unified longing for the things of the world. I want to draw unnecessary distinctions, of course, to make the path of my life easier to justify. I want to point to the hover of the dragonfly over still water and say, *Science regards the dance, poetry the dancer,* though the reversal of this statement would not

violate either science or poetry. I want to say, *Science uses;
art rejoices,* but that is idiotic, for both do both or they are
not hitting on all their cylinders. What *is* the difference
between science and art? Well, that one is taught in science class, the other in art class. Before I am lashed for
flippancy let me insist that I mean exactly that. I believe
they are different because we are taught that they are different, and given different strategies to realize the power of
each. When I first heard poetry I thought I was hearing
data. I thought that the men whose faces appeared on the
pages with their poems had made discoveries, as men find
lost cities or new configurations of molecules, and that
the poems were the records of their discoveries. I wish no
one had ever talked me out of that impression.

I remember clearly first becoming aware of both art and
science as material removed from the background noise
of existence, and of their reconcilable but peculiar properties, and that it happened in one instant.

Born with pulmonary stenosis, I spent a chunk of my
childhood visiting doctors. At the time I write of I was
four years old, a date verified by clippings of the event that
our hometown newspaper found somehow feature-worthy.
The headline read, "Boy Licks Heart Ailment at Four,"
and though untrue, it made me a fourth-magnitude local
media star for a brief time. Generally I played in the waiting rooms while my parents consulted with the cardiolo-
gists over electrocardiogram readouts. For two or three
years I was America's most thorough, if reluctant, con-
sumer of *Highlights for Children* magazine.

All medical waiting rooms featured reproductions of
Impressionist landscapes, on the theory, I suppose, that

they broadcast serenity. Otherwise, one office had little
to recommend it over another to a boy: a few games with
pieces missing that you couldn't play by yourself anyway;
a children's Bible with a vivid Moses-wielding-the-tablets
cover, but an interior crayoned over by urchins less well-
brought-up than oneself; a receptionist who'd chat for a
while, but insisted eventually on getting back to work.
After riffling through the picture magazines, nervous energy led me back to the Impressionist reproductions on
the peach-and-cream walls. Once my eyes found their
mark, they would not be torn away. The paintings repre-
sented how things looked, but *were not* how things looked,
not to me, anyway. You could tell this one was meant to
be a river and overarching trees, but not quite that, not
just that. The people were more shimmery and indistinct
even than the trees and the river. Why? Were they moving
faster? Did the artist like them less? Why were things ambiguous? Why did the scene look so much like what anyone would see standing on the same spot, and yet not, as
though at the last instant it had willed itself into something irreproducible?

It was that word, "irreproducible," that signaled the
difference between these trees and what I would find in
a field guide to the trees. Of course I didn't know the
word then, but I knew the concept. A bird in an osier
bush was always the same bird. Everyone who saw it
would think so. But with a bird in the shrubbery by that
iridescent river, I didn't think it would work the same way.
The painting disturbed me. It was something grown
up and, partially because of its location high up on the
wall, untouchable, holy. It was a secret, but a gaudy, showy
one that wanted to be seen all the time. It filled me with

longing and resentment. On the river a man and a woman in a blinding white dress glided in a boat that was maybe gray and maybe, because of the reflection of the river, the subtlest of greens.

Somebody made this. If somebody made it, then *how* they made it could be figured out.

I stared.

The receptionist gave thanks for a few moments of silence.

Eventually the doctor summoned me into the inner office to hear what they had been deciding about me and my heart surgery. I wasn't interested in that. I wanted to talk about the painting.

In the consultation room, Mother and Father sat with smiles glued to their faces. This itself was an ambiguous sign. The doctor lifted me into a vast leather chair beside his desk, where he summarized what was to happen to me. The surface of the desk was a gleam of dark glass, and on a little stand, reflected in the glass, rested a plaster model of the heart. I couldn't read the label, but I knew instantly what it was, and I was in love. It rendered the two-lobed pink frivolities of Valentine's cards preposterous. Its surface sank into chambers, some violet-blue, some scarlet, crisscrossed with slim paths of vessels of the same brilliance. To be told that within me I possessed the original of this treasure was almost unbearable delight. That my model was faulty and needed to be opened and worked upon was a triviality, like a knock in the engine of a vintage Rolls. I asked if I could put my hands into the chambers, and the doctor said I could. He called them auricles and ventricles. These were instantly my favorite words.

While I boy-handled the plaster heart, the doctor

explained the operation. It was a thoughtful gesture, but my interest was limited by the knowledge that adults would do what they wanted, to me or to anybody else, and though they might ask my opinion, it wouldn't matter very much.

I said, "This isn't real."

The doctor answered, "No, it's a model. Do you understand—"

"Yes. Mine looks just like this?"

"Yes."

He guided my finger to the pulmonic valve, where my trouble was. It was beautiful. Someone would touch my heart like that, my real heart in living scarlet and purple, as I now touched the plaster model.

At that instant I recognized that the painting in the waiting room and the plaster heart were the same. They were objects made to be like something else in the world, but not to take their place, not to be like them *exactly.* The space between identity and similarity was precisely the point. That space was where all the magic dwelt. The doctor put my two hands together to show how big my heart was. The plaster heart was as big as my head. In the waiting room, the painting contained a river and trees and people and a boat, and yet I could carry it away if it were lifted down to me.

Here was magic. You didn't just have to *know* the world. You could change it, too. You could make it bigger, smaller, brighter; you could make it last. It was a power hitherto unsuspected, and I desired it profoundly. I should say I desired *them* profoundly, for I perceived that, though painting and plaster model *did* the same thing, they didn't *want* the same thing. Plaster heart wished to convey information.

Painting aimed to provoke a response. One presented, the other insinuated.

Children are Puritans. The intention of the plaster heart seemed so much cleaner that I thought I'd made my choice. I would be a scientist. An inappropriate but pleasant match, I carried it on faithfully to the threshold of maturity, where the choice reversed itself so gradually that I didn't notice it until all was accomplished. It would be a mistake to think that the distinction between the two lay in subject matter, in the fact that one was "science" and the other "art." The distinction lay purely with me, that I should decide at last the response should mean more than understanding.

It still shocks me to want several things more than I want to understand. Impressionist reproduction and plaster model of the heart both moved me. I am a poet rather than a scientist because my desire, before comprehension, before wisdom, was to move them in return.

～

One gleans details from an unnecessary ledger: the first art—the cave paintings of Altamira, the Rhine Venuses—is perfect and eternal. Yesterday's science is quaint.

The "mistakes" of great artists create unsuspected worlds. The mistakes of science are flushed down the drain.

Some fine artists—Flaubert, Schoenberg, Seurat, Joyce—think like scientists. The greatest scientists think like artists. Theoretical physicists evaluate unverifiable hypotheses according to whether they are "beautiful" or "elegant." That it is beautiful provides our best hope that it is true.

Among scientists and among artists are those who reject moral responsibility. An artist who does so may still be entertaining, even exquisite, if in eternity inconsequential. A scientist who does so is a mad enchanter, heroic and horrible.

The power of science must be limited by what science knows. The power of art increases with mystery. When the power of science exceeds its understanding, the result is monsters: the hydrogen bomb, genetic engineering. When the power of art exceeds its understanding, the result is masterpieces: *King Lear, The Garden of Earthly Delights.*

Scientists live longer than artists. This is a statistic. Most scientists are happier than most artists. This is a theory.

Artists capture the human imagination more firmly and permanently than scientists. Imagine a Broadway show about Lyell, a movie about Agassiz, an opera about chemists living in a garret on the Left Bank. Even exceptions, such as Einstein, are honored more for the mystic in them than for the scientist. In the words of Elizabeth Bishop, "We'd rather have the iceberg than the ship, though it meant the end of travel."

To choose art over science at last is to long for power so great and transfiguring as to be useless in everyday life, on the chance that, in some time remote and in some necessity undreamed of, it might redeem the world. Remember that the highest of created beings are the seraphim. Their sole employment is to cry out, *HOLY!*

The Rhubarb Patch

I T DIDN'T RAIN IN BALTIMORE the first month I lived
there. Each day sailed over Chesapeake Bay bright and
metallic as a coin, departed inland with the flat purple of
paulownia flowers. I'd never lived near the sea before. I
could smell it, salty, sweet, not altogether clean. I'd just
left Hiram, where woods and farms began at the dormitory door, so my attention to the natural world was keen,
not to mention, at that time, obsessive. I saw a Baltimore
that most tourists and many citizens ignore: the groves of
tree of heaven rooted in living brickwork, the clouds of
gulls afloat between dump and bay, the festoons of wiste-
ria that turn upper Charles Street into the May robe of an
emperor. I looked for old friends among the trees and birds,
so as not to feel quite so far off from everything I'd known.
New things appeared, too. I never had seen a cockroach
until I got my apartment on Baltimore Street. There they
were the dominant fauna. I was exhausted after my first
couple of hours smashing them on the walls and floors,
and simply gave up—simply, as most people do, stopped
seeing them. They are not unlovely, actually. If there were
just one, or two, or twenty . . .

If you rose early you could see raccoons cross North

Charles deep within the city. They hurried home from a night of foraging, trying to beat the traffic, humping between mansions with their wily eyes to sleep their days away inches from the fangs of family dogs. The trees were alive with crows. I knew crows from Ohio, but these seemed smarter, more like the sly corbies of the Scots ballads than the black flecks in Midwestern landscapes.

I arrived in Baltimore in August. My stipend at the University didn't begin until the middle of September. Institutions plan things this way to starve their supplicants into gratitude. What I owned was jammed into the back of third-hand moon-colored Toyota station wagon. I had no friends, no idea how to manage alone. Everyone said it was the next step, the breaking free from former things. I'd been a student fifteen years; becoming a *graduate* student sounded inevitable. If I could do something else with my expensive education, no one had volunteered what.

Fear of the side roads of a strange city kept me hugging the main drags. I sat in the motel, running my finger down the thickest lines of my map of greater Baltimore, calling the numbers of the apartment-for-rent ads I thought I could reach safely. This procedure landed me in ghetto digs on Baltimore Street, my landlady assuring me in a torrent of Anglo-Yiddish that it was near the university. It *was* near the university hospital, and needed to be, after the danger and riot of its downtown nights. The story beneath me was occupied by prostitutes. Through the holes in my kitchen floor I could hear their conversations with their customers, sad and tender, like mothers comforting their injured children. Handsome men stood on the street

shouting at each other all night, as though being handsome weren't enough, as though if they stopped shouting
for an instant their turf and their voices and their lives
would be swallowed up.

The whores opened their door when they heard me on
the stairs. They smiled and closed the door when I continued up without having given the sign. I wasn't for them,
even though I wanted a little to be.

My street windows were shattered and held together
with tape. They sported the dings of bullet holes. Mrs.
Stein, the landlady, said, "Don't du vorry, vee get dem fixed
right now." She and I clearly meant different things by the
phrase "right now." But I thought it was okay. I thought
Baltimore was so far south I wouldn't have to worry about
winter. In a crisis I could gather the kitten-sized cock-
roaches for a living blanket between me and the blast.

Sleeping proved difficult. I rose every fifteen minutes
to see if the latest noise was someone breaking into my car.
If I had to park out of sight of my empty windows, I went
downstairs, stood in the street and looked. I thought my
newness made me vulnerable. I thought Baltimore Street
would be out to get the college kid, though if anything the
opposite was true. Everyone was kind. They recognized I
had no part either in their lives or their torment. The handsome violent men stopped shouting when I came out under
city starlight to check my car. They said, "It's all right, kid,
we'll look after you." That I didn't have the courage to believe them doesn't mean they weren't dead serious.

Lying awake listening to the din of life and anger, I
made grand resolutions about how profitable the experience would be, things that would sound fine in a biography

years later had I stuck to them. But after a few nights on
Baltimore Street I went apartment hunting, found a place
far north on Beaumont Avenue with a retired professor
named Bern Briggs, after the city in Switzerland where he
was born.

Bern's second wife, Minna, of his old age when they
were both withered and cautious, met me at the doors and
said, "I don't know. I just don't know."

Need made me bold. I pushed past her into the room
and set my suitcase down. The claim was laid. She accepted
the *fait accompli,* maybe fearful of me there in the morning light, yet wringing her hands and chanting, *I don't
know,* to the Spirit of Hesitancy hovering over her knick-
knacked rooms. The Briggs were extreme—even infernal—
fussbudgets, but nearer to what I was used to than the
whores and chieftains of Baltimore Street.

I drove back to Mrs. Stein to ask for my deposit. She
stooped vulturelike amid second-hand ladles and dented
colanders in a dingy shop lifted bodily from the Warsaw
Ghetto of forty years before. I told her I had to leave. Told
her I had to go home. They were lies, but things I knew
how to say in German, which she had understood well
enough when I took the apartment. Now she pretended
not to understand. She whipped her head from side to side
as though I were doing her harm. She raised her sleeve so I
could see the blue numbers tattooed, each curve and dis-
coloration declaring she had suffered enough in the camps.
So I left my deposit to comfort her, moved northward into
the upright urban neighborhoods surrounding Loyola and
Notre Dame, Catholic schools deep in the shade of the
magnolias, where nuns dragoon passersby into carrying

their groceries and Jesuits pass with the sure stride of the omniscient.

I knew nobody and was penniless. Carrying my gear to the fussbudgets' second floor I had to stop and hunker down on the steps every few loads, shaky from having eaten nothing. I didn't mind it so much—the sensation of physical privation interested me, an exploration of an unsuspected interior kingdom. But it also left me lightheaded and cranky, which militated against the good impression I wanted to make.

One night Mrs. Briggs gave me their unfinished portion of take-out fried chicken. I ate so greedily I spent the evening sick over the toilet, finishing as empty as I had begun.

Begging occurred to me as a viable solution. I didn't know how to do it, so I stood outside a café near campus looking as forlorn as I could with my tanned skin and graduate student sleekness. The people this strategy worked on were gay men, who bought me drinks, which was worse than nothing.

Maybe it was the lightheadedness of hunger, but I became religious again, walking back and forth between Hopkins and Beaumont Avenue under the buzzing street lights asking God to make me a saint. I am not sure I knew what I meant by this. My guess is I thought a saint was someone who could comfort a person as miserable as I.

Classes began. In the seminar room we acquired the credentials of hauteur. We were a school with a lofty name and an affected disdain for the central passions of the discipline we claimed as our own. Nobody really liked literature that much, or if they did, were ashamed of admitting

it. If anyone was so naive as to ask a question, the rest of
the room struggled to find a way to make the question look
ridiculous. This academic language was foreign to me, the
language of distance and avoidance. I couldn't speak it,
couldn't bring myself to want to learn. I took it personally.
They would never love me as the professors back home
had, when we innocently thought of ourselves as seekers
and teachers. Now that we were professionals nobody
loved anybody. I would not be their golden boy. "Jilted,"
was the word, but it remained unsaid.

I sit in a seminar room at Johns Hopkins, in Baltimore.
I'm too young, too—*something* to be a graduate student.
I'm lonely, homesick, unready for the levels of profession-
alism and cynicism I feel around me. I go home every night
wondering if I could really be as stupid as every incident
makes me feel. Professors discourse brilliantly, but with that
air of a trapeze act which does not quite equal love of learning. My colleagues respond to their questions, laugh at
their quips with laugh-track regularity. I sit like someone
from a foreign country, trying to take it all in, compre-
hending everything that is said but not, somehow, to what
end it is being said.

Late afternoons, a mockingbird beats to the lilac shrub
outside the classroom window. He waits for the branch
to stop quivering, and begins to sing, with infinite, liquid
invention, with a satiric wit that mocks, sweetly, the drone
of erudition issuing from the room. I couldn't be the only
one hearing him, but no one else is looking, no one else
is the least disturbed or distracted. Perhaps I am the only
one *needing* to hear. I listen with eyes narrowed. I hope

Professor Wasserman thinks all that concentration is for him and Wordsworth.

The first time he comes, I believe it is a mistake. The second time, too good to be true. The remarkable thing is that I forget him from day to day, so his advent in the lilac bush is ever a surprise, ever a fresh delight. As he arrives, like clockwork, one afternoon upon another, I begin to understand he is a special grace. He comes to give me peace; he comes to give peace to anyone who listens, but I am the only one listening. Like Siegfried, I had bathed in dragon's blood, and fathomed every note.

It didn't hurt that the course was the Romantic poets, and one afternoon we considered Keats's nightingale, doing for him what my mockingbird did for me, opening the casement window onto the foam of perilous seas in fairy lands, forlorn. I waited for Professor Wasserman to close the window on the bird—which was, after all, quite loud—but it was hot late summer, and he never did. Or perhaps the professor was listening. Perhaps he was speaking through the back of his head to the ecstatic bird, *They may not hear you, but I do, old friend.*

When Columbus sails around Hispaniola, he reports hearing the song of the "nightingale," by which he means the mockingbird. Mad poet Christopher Smart writes an "Ode to a Virginia Nightingale," by which he, again, indicates the mockingbird. His mockingbird had hurt its wing and been nursed back to health by a beautiful lady. Walt Whitman uses the mockingbird as an image of the human soul in that greatest of American poems, "Out of the Cradle Endlessly Rocking," picturing a widowed male bird flying out over the depths of the sea, calling to his lost mate. This poem puzzled me as a child growing up in Ohio, for I, who had a sharp eye for such things, had never seen one, and there Whitman was on Long Island, which looks on the map to be north of Ohio, awash in pairs of them, apparently of a lyrical and tragical turn. I saw my first in a cemetery in Pikesville, Maryland, while I was heading toward the debacle of my first graduate student career, already alluded to. I must have prophesied it all in my heart, for I had gone to the cemetery, which abutted my motel, in order to work out the misery which at that point was apparently unfounded, but fully real. Instead, I watched the mockingbirds under the blue blaze of afternoon light. My life has never since then for more than a few weeks been without them. They have never failed to distract me from misery, or to put a seal on joy.

For a while I traveled in circles that were big on Spirit Guides. A Spirit Guide is an animal one should look to as a sort of spiritual tutor, whose motions and destiny have something to do with one's own. My martial arts instructor cruelly suggested that my Spirit Guide was the Energizer Bunny, the drum-banging, indestructible toy used on TV to advertise a brand of batteries. Another in our party suggested the wolverine. These comments, aimed at my locally famous relentlessness, though I could understand them, did not strike me as being exactly on the money. Choosing for myself, I would choose the mockingbird. Because he tries everything. Because he sings from the highest branch, and sings alone.

I sit reading beside an osier bush in the cemetery. I've sat
so long and still that the bush's resident hermit thrush
forgets I'm here. He begins to sing. I've heard thrushes,
but never before ten inches from my ear. Like a river of
bells, he flows and chimes at once. Like some great organ,
he seems never to need to breathe. He gurgles a line, stops,
reconsiders, alters the passage, sings through the new version twice, to make it right. Then he launches into variations at once florid and austere. It is so sweet—and so
surprisingly loud—that I want to say, with some sickly
Romantic poet, that it is too much to bear. But I bear it,
my book dropped facedown in the grass. Venus shines
out, and the thrush launches from his branch to hunt. He
pauses, stares at me, the beads of his eyes asking what present I can give him in return.

The answer is, *Nothing.*

So, afternoons, the mockingbird sang outside the seminar
room window. I pretended that was enough.

After class I staggered light-headed from fasting through
the streets, singing. Singing kept me alert. It kept me from
thinking about how hungry I was. Besides, people are not
attracted to miserable people, and I meant to be attractive.
I wanted strangers to stop the car, call to me, take me in,
tell me to forget the disappointing thing I'd come for and
have a life unsuspected.

At last someone directed me to the Hopkins Student
Center, Levering Hall. I hadn't known there was one.

"What's the matter, Bud?" a classmate said, catching me
trembling in the draft from the hall. He looked like he
might have money to lend. I told the truth.

"I'm hungry."

He did not catch the hint. Instead he told me how to find the student center cafeteria. Futile though it was, I went through with it because he stood watching from the stairs to make sure I found the way.

I went in. Carried along by the tide of food-acquiring I stood in line, chose the immense chef salad I would have chosen had there been money.

In the Levering Hall cafeteria the condiment table stood beyond the cash register, and if you were desperately hungry or very bold you could select a chef salad, carry it past the check-out girl, add your dressing, proceed into the dining area as though the complexities of bleu cheese ladling had made tendering payment slip your mind. This could be done also with hamburgers and mustard, but that sort of food seemed vaguely recreational to me, and if I were going to steal, I meant it to be a matter of necessity.

The first time I did this it was an accident. From then on, it was art. The first time was wholly inadvertent. I was seated, gobbling, before realizing what I had done. Afterwards it was calculation—or to put a better light on it, acquiescence to an unlooked-for Providence.

Sometimes twice a day I pulled my chef salad scam: once at lunch, the busiest time for the cafeteria, when employees hadn't leisure to watch individual customers, and once in early evening when the night-school students took over and the atmosphere was relaxed and homey, the employees mellow to the brink of narcosis. Chef salads comprised my intake on those days, along with the crackers that sat in a plastic vat and which custom suggested I could have as many of as I wanted. The diet suited me. I looked lean and dangerous. I looked like the sort of person who stole salad as a courtesy, to keep the city safe from worse things of which he was capable.

I'll save the history of Baltimore and me for another time, only to say that when summer came again I was faced with the necessity of living without a stipend from the university. I was certainly not going to go home. I figured the gods would not let me return to scamming salads. Unlooked-for succor came from Bern Briggs, my landlord, who made a few phone calls, and I was taken onto the staff of Koinonia, a commune in the horsey, rolling countryside north of Baltimore. The commune offered classes to paying residents, and one of them was nature study, and what was I but a "professional naturalist," by virtue of really having been paid to drag kids through the scruffy woods of Ohio?

Koinonia was no gaggle of granola fantastics gathered for a season under the stars. Since 1949, when it was established by Laubach literacy missionaries, it had occupied a mansion called Gramercy, that had once been owned by a senator, if I remember the stories right. On one side of us dwelt the Calverts, of Maryland's founding family. On the other side dwelt the great soprano, Rosa Ponselle. I had sung for Ponselle's company, the Baltimore Opera, and lay sometimes on the golden hillside behind her house, gnawing blades of grass and wondering if it would profit me to wander down and reintroduce myself. "Hi, I was the twenty-ninth chorus boy in black face in *Aida*. Perhaps you would like to help me establish a career?" Lying on the hillside long enough attracted a spiral of vultures above my sprawled form, circling, looking for signs of movement. That seemed, at the time, emblematic of my life.

While I was lying on Rosa Ponselle's hillside, dreaming,

I was being introduced to everybody as the "community naturalist." This was mildly embarrassing, but I hit the books, learning, learning, and though someone always knew something I didn't, the sum total of my natural history knowledge at that time was pretty impressive, I thought. Enough to lead nature hikes and point out the stuff that was even mildly interesting, mimic a bird-song here and there, dig a few roots and brew a little tea.

A heavy Quaker presence pervaded the place, which meant, among other things, that the long-time Koinonians said very little unless they had something to say. Though I was hired to give residents and visitors "a sense of the natural world," it was difficult for me to know whether I was doing so. "Feedback" is not a concept widely honored among Quakers. Those who had their own sense of the natural world already smiled and nodded and left me undecided as to whether I were being insightful and revelatory or simply a babbling nuisance. Our students and visitors, who might have no sense of the natural world whatever, were equally silent, though out of stupefaction, and when they spoke it was often to observe, "You could be making all this stuff up and we would never know," which was quite true, actually.

Koinonia was a sort of paradise, had my life been free enough from agitation to take proper note. Mulberries overhung Honey Brook. A wild tangle of strawberries clung to a south slope, where they could be harvested twice a day in season. Beehives sat on posts beside the bean rows, a hum like electric wiring forever alive in the shadow of the trees. It was the sort of place where a plowed furrow would be turned aside to save a single blossoming cardinal flower, where the whole community would be summoned before supper to contemplate that single torch of red blossom as a meditation, a grace before table. It was the sort of place where someone would bring you a present in a jar covered by a white cloth. You would remove the cloth and find, wound around inside the jar, a young milk snake, in wheat and cream checkerboard, bright as Eden. When I poured it into my hand, it coiled contentedly, as though the hand were a rock warmed by the sun.

It was the sort of place where you would be wakened from sleep by something hammering in threes in the mimosa tangle outside your window. It was, of course, the Carolina wren, many times louder and bolder than its tiny size would seem to allow. The commune folk said the wren was crying, *Rise and Shine! Rise and Shine!* but I found in him such vehemence that I heard, *Go to hell! Go to hell!*—the emphasis, like a country preacher's, migrating through the syllables.

In addition to gallantry, the little wren possesses several qualities I prize in any animal. He is not too proud. He builds his home in the scruffy tangles by the driveway, leaving lordly oak and tulip to others. He is valiant. The she-wren scans from the eaves of my porch for the neighbors' taffy cat, hopping from one stick foot to the other in anticipation, then, seeing her quarry, power-dives, rattling like a snake as the poor beast blunders into range. The he-wren is mechanical. I go to my car at morning; he flutters out from under it, as if caught tinkering with the joints and shafts. He is loyal. He and his mate stay the winter, *hammerklaviering* the same resonant threes through sleet and blizzard after *tout le monde* has lightwinged south.

Two pairs of Carolina wrens nested within bellowing distance of my bed at Koinonia, one in a rotting log pile directly under my window, another in the raspberry patch on the open slope beyond the encircling conifers. As with the strawberries, the raspberries needed picking twice a day in prime yield weather, and working the wrens' row was a test of mettle. You wondered when you'd be startled witless by a ball of fury exploding inches from your face. Nor could meaningful accommodation be reached with the residents of the berry patch, as the critical distance altered with each picking. Sometimes you could pluck berries overhanging the nest like old-fashioned light fixtures. At other times the birds met you, tails bobbing with incipient battle-fury, at the very edge of the garden. Surely nobody is afraid of a wren, yet for six feet on either side of the nest hung raspberries, bursting ripe, unharvested.

Fridays the Koinonians left their regular tasks and were given special jobs that had come up during the week, which were often as unlike their normal undertakings as possible. The gardeners might balance ledgers. The nurse might can berries. The naturalist—I—was given, one bright day, the rhubarb patch to put to order. Now the fact is, I had not seen a rhubarb patch before, and when it was shown to me I understood why. It was a rectangle of ground so overgrown with weeds that though rhubarb could be discovered within it, it was by no means the dominant flora.

I must take a step or two back in order to explain why this is important. As I might have implied earlier, it had been a very trying year, the most disastrous of my life till then, and to add to the bitterness, the first that had not been aglow with a child's innocent happiness. I was not only annihilated; I was taken utterly by surprise.

Nor was the communal experience working out especially well. Though Marian the Nurse, Dick the Organic Gardener, Helen the Garden Sprite, Ella the Cook, and a dozen other residents, were among the most exemplary and upright people in my experience, they were not alone under the red oaks. One of the important members of the commune was the first evil person I'd ever met, and the interest I had in observing and learning his ways was rather overwhelmed by dread and sorrow. Organized, concentrated, and cunning intention to make things go wrong was new to me, and though I was not utterly blindsided by it, as I had been by the disasters of the preceding winter, I had no idea how to face it. It was stronger than I. It had—and used—the power to make me look like an idiot. Crossing the center of the commune by night, one experienced a wall, invisible, perhaps, but fully palpable, dividing the rest of us from the dwelling of that unhappy man. I am not a fanciful person. I do not believe in UFOs or ghosts, and would not have believed *this* if it were just told to me by someone else, if I had not felt it myself. Being so without context, it preyed ceaselessly on my mind.

Sunday night one of the students, Kay, knocked at my door. Kay was crying, and very frightened. She said "I came here because yours was the only light on." I went outside with her and saw that Koinonia was a blaze of light, one in almost every inhabited window. I thought it best not to mention that. Kay had been trying to do the composting, which was her task that evening, but something had frightened her by the compost pit. The pit stood at the edge of the upper garden, where the berries and fruit trees were. It was a large cement and brick structure, like an oven, with an extremely heavy cast-iron door. I had assumed Kay

wanted me to lift the door for her. It was put on to keep
the raccoons from getting into the compost, and many of
the women could not lift it. Why she was so upset about
asking me to lift the door I couldn't understand until we
neared the upper garden. A terrific banging and crashing
smote the night air. There was not a breath of wind, and
yet when we got close enough, we saw that the noise was
the heavy cast-iron door of the compost pit banging open
and closed as though it were a shutter in a gale. Each time
it hit the structure, bits of brick and mortar flew into the
surrounding vegetation. I walked close enough to determine that there was no animal—it would have had to have
been a bear—manipulating it. Closer than that neither of
us would go. I'd never had the experience of being literally
nailed to the spot with terror. Dick Falkenstein, the head
gardener, once an agricultural missionary to China, the
silent Quaker sage, appeared out of the darkness, brushed
past Kay and me and took the iron door by the handle. It
jerked his frail body once, then slammed shut with the
loudest bang of all. He looked at us in the gathering starlight and said, "Something has to be done."

Surely to God, yes, but if by me, the gods were slow
in telling me what, or how.

So this brings us back to the rhubarb patch. It was
Friday after the Sunday night of the haunted compost.
Dick asked me to bring the rhubarb rectangle up to standards. I was as empty inside as I had ever been—no,
worse—I was empty inside, as I had *never* before been.
I was the superhero kid handed his first string of defeats,
his first taste of kryptonite. I needed something to concentrate on, something that had nothing to do with me.

I started at the northwest corner of the rhubarb planting, working toward the southeast, which, by the way, kept the compost pit in my line of sight. I pulled the weeds with determined precision, pushing the tender green rhubarb away with the back of my hand, beating the roots against the ground to clean them of dirt, pulling the white grubs away and tossing them to the grackles who waited for just such an offering, making sure the precious red earthworms, the soil-makers, sank back into the loam. My knees and my bare chest made contact first with the leaves of the patch and then, as the patch cleared, with the dirt itself, soft and warm, like a bed badly made but fragrant and welcoming. When I came to poison ivy I made a glove of leaves and wrapped it around the vine, pulled, walked each vine individually to the pit, standing in blazing summer light now, without terror. I worked through break. I accepted the iced tea that was brought to me, but kept working. Late in the afternoon I stopped, stood, looked back at my handiwork. There was a rectangle of dark brown soil, studded at regular intervals with the unfolding hands-at-prayer of the rhubarb, red at the base, working toward the palest sunstruck chrysoprase. It was a thing of beauty. It was perfection.

That night, supper meditation was my rhubarb patch, partially to celebrate a job well done, partially to take in the simple elegance of a few plants in a space of dirt, a Maryland Zen garden that would transmute into pies and cobbler before the leaves were golden.

I was not proud of myself, exactly. I was *strengthened*. I had done something perfectly. After I was through with it, the rhubarb patch could not have been better and still remained itself. Nothing was left undone, nothing taken too far. Maybe I have done a few perfect things since, but not many, and the rhubarb patch lingers in memory as the first that was *necessary,* that I could not have endured without.

The Hosts of the Air

AFFINITY WITH CERTAIN CREATURES is a free gift, unrefusable, generally unprofitable, precious beyond platinum. My friend David Factor can take you into the woods behind the college biology station in Hiram, Ohio, on a spring morning, and show you fifteen species of warbler, all but a few perfectly invisible and inaudible to your own unaided senses. You'll have difficulty crediting such abundance until you follow with your binoculars an imaginary line shot from the end of David's pointing finger into the understory, gradually, laboriously zeroing in on the tiny living whistle box he sensed yards off. Hiking with him in a space no larger than a suburban backyard, on two spring mornings, I saw most of the warblers I am ever likely to see, including the elusive mourning warbler, which Audubon considered rare and of which its very discoverer saw but one. Mr. Factor claims to pull this trick by meticulous knowledge of the warblers' individual songs, a claim he makes plausible by imitating them to, so far as my ears can discern, perfection. I have never asked David how he came by this skill, for I think I know what he'll say. He'll say, "I don't know. It just came. It was something I was always good at."

Like I said, a blessing, a free gift. Knowledge of warblers is a form of grace descended through—as is the case with all forms of grace—no virtue of the recipient.

As a birder I have my talents and my shortcomings: bad eyes, good ears, impatience, imagination, a general understanding of where birds are likely to be. Nevertheless, warblers have always been excruciating. I've seen my share, but seldom on purpose. My first parula warbler crashed into my screen door in Ohio, and lay dazed in my hand before coming to and fluttering off in a ruffle of lazuli indignation. A black-throated blue rode into a convenience store in North Carolina one Easter Sunday, in the hands of a woman who had come to buy kerosene. It too had crashed into some architectural feature—I won't comment on the intelligence of something that can blunder into a *house*—and it too revived when she took it outside and laid it on the sidewalk. A migrating prairie warbler rested overnight in brush against my window when I lived in a converted chicken coop at the foot of Mount Pisgah. Some I saw while jogging (me, not them). A male Blackburnian perched in the branch of a spruce inches from my face, like an Egyptian god with the sun's disk for a head. A yellow-throat landed on my boot while I was following a covey of gadwalls. A chat exploded in a red oak ten feet from my face, looking the other way, insolently oblivious to my presence and the heat of my desire for him.

So, the Grace of Warblers comes sporadically to me, though other sorts of grace flow sufficiently to permit a conviction of ornithological salvation. If I go to the water, I will see a heron. Period. Great blue, mostly, but also green, black-crowned night, reddish egret, the species changing, like the stars, as one goes south. Taking a piss in the woods around Maddy's Pond, I realize I am being scrutinized by a green heron, looking at that angle less green than verdigris-and-gold, with electric orange legs that look like they were borrowed from somebody else. I bought my Ford because during the test drive I was trying to watch a great blue heron stalking and freezing at the edge of the river, while the salesman reeled off the car's virtues. "Yes," I kept saying, "yes," until the deed was done.

A vixen whelped in the rocks behind the pool at the townhouse complex where I used to live. Mornings, she brought her pups down to sun and to keep tabs on the human activity around the pool. The vixen was red, the pups red at legs and tail, but with silver saddles across their narrow backs. Human mothers brought their children up to swim, then stopped to watch the foxes, holding the children's hands, trying to instill at once both courage and caution. Mother and child, vixen and pups, each sent out their signals, each mother whispering, *Watch and learn.*

When I lived in Exeter, New Hampshire, I'd walk evenings to a wharf at the head of the Squamscott to visit the resident blue heron. He put in an appearance every night— but then, so did I, so maybe he was there to look at me. If the wharf happened to be vacant when I arrived, I'd wait for him to flap back from hunting and land there under hunched shoulders, a spirit at once infinitely aged and profoundly droll.

All herons are comic. Not *comedians* like chickadees or crows, but comic. Like a *zaftig* dowager in a Marx brothers farce, they sail on unaffected by the wake of hilarity they shed around themselves. This is a function of flawless personal gravity. Human sages and prophets are funny in the same way. You do not laugh at them, but *because* of them, because of their imperial solemnity, at once so lovely and so incongruous. On Plum Island, Massachusetts, I knew where to find a concentration of black-crowned night herons. They are the Cary Grants of birds, at once funny and elegantly handsome. They stand in shallow water feeling about in the mud with one claw, like a man fumbling for his lunch in a sack, while keeping his head up in the conversation.

If I enter a wood of any size I will find a pileated woodpecker. Rather, it will find me. I hate saying "it," but I can't tell male from female among pileateds unless they're mating, which I have also seen them do, in Corkscrew Swamp in Florida, with a vehemence that harmonized with the flaring red crests. Experienced birders have seen their first pileated with me, amazed that one so haphazard should lure such a wonder out of the shadows. I tell them it is not my fault.

On Christmas Day I hike from Chestnut Cove on the Blue Ridge Parkway to Sleep Gap, and back, over hill open by the bareness of winter to all distances. When I stop, the branches quicken with nuthatches, chickadees, titmice, downy woodpeckers, and, most hugely of all, the great pileated woodpeckers, Yule birds in their vivid black and red. There are at least three individuals, two seemingly a pair, the other challenging them with hysterical Gatling-gun calls from the periphery of their territory. When I disturb them, they drop low, so as not to leave a silhouette against the sky. They scream and flap; they have heaven to themselves.

Most bird guides call the pileated silent and secretive. I don't feature *this* at all. Are they bombastic and demonstrative only around me? Is that part of the Grace of Woodpeckers? I locate the birds by sound, by the maniacal, mechanical scream loosed at occasionally quite close range. Woody Woodpecker, the cartoon personality, is probably meant to be a pileated. The flaming red crest is right, and in Woody's irritating laugh (which as a child I learned to mimic to perfection) we have at once a diminishment and a celebration of the pileated's blood-chilling scream—with wolf-howl and loon-cry, the essential voice of the wilderness. The pileated's other sound is the noise of an ax. If you hear an ax falling in the woods with almost-but-not-quite-human force and regularity, and you scan the forest floor without seeing anybody, look up. Watch the chips fly.

Christmas Day in the mountains, and each surface wears its ornament of lichen: green, blue-green, pale yellow. The sky possesses the glowering luminosity that comes before storms. A drop of two degrees will bring snow. High on the ridge, a twisted, giant oak is shot through by a straight sapling. To complete the composition, someone has hung a beer can on a long string fifteen feet from the ground, comically endearing, oddly lovely and in place, nature and art in a single glance.

Unsated, I hike again on the second day of Christmas, the Feast of Saint Stephan, proto-martyr. I move from Beaverdam Gap to Bent Creek Gap. On Young Pisgah Mountain—the very top of the world until you get to Pisgah glowering to the southwest—stands a foundation of cement block, aborted, tumble-down, littered with those ubiquitous signs of human life, plastic soda bottles, which shall outlast all visible things, save the mountain itself. The area around the broken tower—if that's what it was—is a trampled glade bristling with brambles and tawny winter grass. In the mortar of the blocks are written names, and the date 1933. It might as well be Machu Picchu for all I knew of its origins and use. That is the reason I cherish the spot so much, and why, after that first discovery, I returned again and again, watching as the configuration and nature of the human debris changed, and the surrounding vegetation remained exactly the same.

Of all earth's creatures, only insects possess true wings; that is, wings that were always wings and never forelimbs. Everything else that has ever taken to the air has by some convulsion of genetic will transfigured itself. Say you are an early Jurassic carnosaur. Your cousins include the greatest terrestrial carnivores of all time, nightmarish *Antrodemus;* bully-boy *Albertosaurus* haunting the foothills of the northern Rockies; that perfection of calamities, *Tyrannosaurus.* You expect the best is over for your clan, not realizing that nature has something further in mind for you. It has happened twice before, and will happen at least once again, but never with such spectacular and various results. Your DNA takes it into its head to leap off the surface of the planet, to rocket into the very air. It hollows you from within, whittles your bones until they're empty as whistles, strutted for support like tiny cathedrals. It speeds up your heart, boils your blood, knocks out your teeth, dissolves away your digits, swells your breastbone, tortures your comfy green scales into feathers, and not *one* kind of feather, but down and secondary and primary, pinion and quill. It miniaturizes, miniaturizes, miniaturizes—except in the case of the ratites, where it makes huge again. It forbids live birth to you forever. It sharpens your eyes beyond the acuity of any mere lizard. You can spot a beetle on a stone from a thousand feet.

Your earliest fossil, *Archaeopteryx,* caused a sensation when someone dug it out of a German limestone quarry, for here appears to be evolution's proof in stone, a transitional form, part bird, part reptile. A chimera. Except that your feathers are so perfect, many think you at first a hoax. Don't biological features have to *develop?* Mustn't there be lousy feathers before there are good feathers? The answer is, no; everything is perfect at once. It may be perfect differently in a generation or so, but no creature is "transitional" in its own conception. To tell Archaeopteryx that he was transitional to swans and hummingbirds would make no more sense than to tell mother Australopithecus that she was just a way-stop on the way to Eve.

Plus, you can fly. You take to the wind in the Mesozoic

morning, land in my locust tree with grass in your beak
for this year's nest. I greet you, stock still behind my window, saying, casually, as though it were the most ordinary
thing in the world, *cardinal!*

I had a parrot once, actually a canary-winged parakeet,
named Capella, after the star. Remembering her power
of flight only in moments of fury or panic, Capella climbed
down from her cage and walked where she would, crossing large rooms to bite the toes of people she disliked, or
to mount beakhold by beakhold onto the shoulders of the
chosen. Often one kicked her across the floor on one's in-
attentive way to the john in the dark of morning. When I
took time to contemplate these occurrences, I recognized
their strangeness. Usually she didn't even bother to squawk
when kicked, and otherwise Capella was a great squawker.
She seemed scarcely to notice, but righted herself and took
off again, jungle-green and undaunted. Change the scale
and you have a sixty-foot giant punting me half a mile. I
believe I would have squawked.

Capella's durability led me to contemplate the skeletons of birds, an engineering triumph to hush the mouths
of the prophets, to bring the suicide down from the ledge.
The girdle is a grass leaf dried and curled; spine's whittled
to a splinter, a thorn; clavicle is a taut hair holding without
weight. Everything's reduced, streamlined, punched
through with air pockets and passageways, honed for flight.
Were we as retooled to house our vaunted brains as the bird
is for its wings, we would be ambulating spheres of skull,
bulged with eyes, nerve-ropes tasting the air. Wings are
power without mass. They are a folded plane, toothpicks
thickened with blood, in good wind, lofting by themselves,

fraught with girder, crossbeam, strut, willing to bear, made to lift; with that furious heart behind them, lighter than air, nimbler than light, ready to hover, veer, power, stoop, home in, evade, ascend. Kick them across the kitchen floor, they gather and leap back. Hurl them into the hurricane, they seize the wind and ride.

Fury is not the cat nor the bear, but the wren. Boldness is the chickadee ripping thistles from the bear's pelt to line its nest, the mockingbird—as I have seen them—snatching grubs from beneath the beating ax. Killdeer leaps before fox and wanton boy, dragging her wing in a mockery of distress, defending her generations. Geese hurl above Everest. Why not higher? Only because the atmosphere thins and refuses to bear. Each day they rise upon the rungs of the wind, take their bit of earth up, insubstantial, indestructible, stopping because the world stops, not their will nor bones.

~

I'm running in my Nike waffles, in the teeth of storm, the trees bending down around me. I could go home where it is safe, scurrying into shelter as everyone else has, but there is such sudden exaltation in the wind, in the coming of the storm. I have never felt that before. I look over my head, and there is a kestrel, fluttering, directly above me, outlined in the yellow light of the tempest. Understanding passes between us like a bolt of electricity. We are both flying in the teeth of storm, for the joy of it.

~

It is spring before the leaves come, sprinkled with hepaticas, furred and lavender in the glades. I am sitting very still, watching a grouse strut and peck. It's been a quarter of an hour; I am an impatient man, and I've seen nearly as much grouse as I need to see. It seems impolite to stir and ruin her breakfast, though—when suddenly a dark shape bullets through the trees. The wings seem much too wide to make it through the branches, but they do. I sit, fascinated. The grouse must see it too, but she stands frozen. The shape hovers over her for an instant, falls, strikes. It is a red-tailed hawk. He covers his prey as though I were a rival predator (which I guess I am), rips her to death, clutches her limp body, lifts heavily back into the air. I crawl to the spot. From a spatter of blood I take two feathers.

I'm farm-sitting between Windham and Garrettsville, Ohio. It is very cold, and each day the liquid space in the center of the farm pond diminishes, though the wild, migratory geese manage to keep a patch of it free by paddling around and around in it. After one night of terrible cold, though, I wake to the sound of barking and of angry geese. I look out the window and see that the farm dogs, friendly mutts who sniff my fingers and whine, have turned into a killer pack. They have something out on the ice. The pond is frozen now, and the geese have gone—except two. One is dive-bombing the dogs from the air. One, curiously, does not move, but extends her neck, hissing at the dogs, flogging at them with her wings. She is getting tired and the dogs are getting closer. I wonder, "Why doesn't she fly?" Then I look at the pond and realize it is frozen solid. Her feet are frozen into the ice. By the time I get my boots on and plow out to the pond, they have gnawed her off at the ankle bones. They are tearing the body apart, and while they're in this mood I have no wish to come near them. The male stands on the pond rim, honking, still trying to distract the dogs, still trying valiantly to save her. He is her mate. Geese mate for life.

Upstate New York: wind had been rolling from the southwest, as though there were a sea there. I was hiking at the two Green Lakes left by the glacier. I heard a lone goose, far beneath the din made by the migrators hurdling overhead. I ran to the sound and saw him rolling across the ground on one good leg and one stiff leg. He'd gotten himself too deep into the thickets to use his wings. Blood stained his breast where it met the hurt leg, a few feathers blown away by a shotgun. He had to get out of the thicket, had to get back into the air. I shouted, "Fox! Dog! Hunter!" but those words didn't move him. I walked close. He rolled to get away. I ran toward him; he ran to get away. I ran him to the lakeshore, where from under the boughs the way was suddenly clear. He beat his wings on the pebbles, on the green water, lifted heavily over the circle of hills, shot off southward without another sound.

For several nights a pair of screech owls have shrieked and shivered in the locust hedge at my window. I say "pair" as a minimal estimation. I haven't actually seen the owls, but I assume that such a variety of disturbing noise cannot be made by one and need not require more than two. That the sound is soft doesn't matter—it is eerie and fills the dark, and might as well be the howling of banshees. It is a sound at once pathetic and appalling, like a very small monster hoping to gain your sympathies.

When I worked at a liquor store in Syracuse, New York, I walked home at night through Thornden Park, a tattered, lovely, grassy space with a very bad after-dark reputation. One, therefore, made it a point of macho honor to drive right through the heart of it at all hours, or at least never to be perceived deliberately going around. I walked through all the time and had never seen anything even vaguely suspicious. It did occur to me, however, that perhaps I lent a legend to the night by my own passing through the park in the deep of night, a scurrying shadow that could be interpreted, from the street, as the form of a desperado.

One night the north end of the park, nearest my house, was flakked by searching flashlights. Madison Street below was lit with police lights turning blue arcs on their turrets.

"What's the matter?" I asked the black space behind one of the flashlights.

"Screaming. Somebody heard screaming up here."

As the officer spoke, he held the light away from my eyes for a moment. Its ray climbed an ancient box elder, where, lined up on a branch like toys on a shelf, sat four screech owls. They fluffed and glared and shifted from claw to tiny claw. They stretched their necks and craned, exactly as I was doing, to get a better look at whoever was looking at them. Before I could redirect the officer's attention upward, the owls glided soundlessly off, one by one. "Good luck," I said, lacking the heart to tell them what, magnified by darkness and the glamour of the night, the screaming was.

Terror of the screech owl's screech diminishes somewhat after one lays eyes on the creature itself. No owl is cuddly, but the small ones are droll, baby-faced, unlikely threats to mammals of our size.

The great owls are another matter. As a child I visited a farm where my father bought dry corn to feed the birds through winter. Across the door of the barn was stretched, cruciform, the white corpse of a shotgunned barn owl. To keep out rats and sparrows, they told me. I thought it would keep out wildcats, with that acre of wing, that smouldering intensity of black eye in the heart-shaped face, formidable even in death.

More intimidating still is the great horned owl, the Halloween owl that really does say, *Who?* with the tone of God on Judgment Day. Hunters claim great horned owls can kill and carry off fawns. I myself have found undigested fox brush in owl pellets, and once the wing of a hawk.

My first great horned appeared years ago, while I played with friends in Goodyear Heights Metropolitan Park in Akron, Ohio. High in a white oak we spied what we assumed to be a squirrel's nest. Being boys, our impulse was to throw something at it, to provoke some action. It was early spring, and heavy jackets impeded our throwing arms somewhat, but at last I got one high enough to nick the dark shape. Instantly it sprouted wings, and with a sepulchral *Who?* glided from the limb above our astonished heads into the deep of the forest. I fell permanently in love.

~

Green Lakes, Upstate New York, a crisp late autumn day after a spectacular cold snap that turned the waters of the north to stone. I walked the lake path with my hands jammed into my pockets. The forest stood so utterly bare that every scurrying rodent, every stay-at-home bird shone in blue-white clarity.

While it was still a way off, I began to scan a brown complication halfway up a tulip poplar tilted over the lake. The mass seemed out of place on the clean outline of the tree. It reminded me of the "squirrel's nests" of my youth, and I walked faster, hoping for an owl, perhaps a snowy, a ghostly presence from the far north. A hundred yards off I knew it was an owl, a big one, a great horned, plain as a hillside. I commenced a cautious approach, stepping with a deliberation difficult for an impatient man, stopping whenever her head swivelled my way. Closer. Closer. Closer. Closer than I'd ever stood to one before. Nearly as close as I'd been to so wild a thing. I couldn't believe my luck.

There's a point at which the dream of approaching wild things, touching them, tasting acceptance lost since Adam, wavers over into unease. We are men. They are beasts. It is our business to stalk, theirs to flee. We are un-comfortable when it turns out otherwise. By those same green lakes one summer I "stalked" a fox in a sun-struck meadow, hoping he would lead me to his den. After let-ting me approach for a few hundred yards, he turned and looked square at me. Assuming it was over anyway, I ap-proached briskly, hoping to get as close as possible before he scurried off. He didn't budge. I took another step. An-other. The wind blew in his ruff, but beyond that, not a muscle stirred, no change of expression on the red muzzle, not even an apparent effort to "freeze." White moths circled his head, but he ignored them to stare straight at me. I'd crept close enough to touch him with my shoe when the horrific word *rabies* formed in my brain. I backed off a mite quicker than I had come. The fox still had not moved.

So, my emotion was not pure delight when I touched the base of the tulip and the owl still had not budged. I gazed up, hand flat over my eyes against the sun and the reflecting glare of the lake ice, and saw that the owl's legs were tangled in wire, and the wire tangled in complica-tions of the tree's body.

I wish to say that my plan formed instantly, but it didn't. It would have been quite possible to say, "Poor thing," and continue prudently on my way. The owl's branch extended over imperfectly frozen ice, which itself lay over— everyone who knows the Green Lakes knows this—incal-culably deep water. Not a tree climber as a boy, I am no better at it now. The two miles to my car was a long way to go with soaked clothing or broken bones. Still, one knows what one can live with, and what one can't, so I began to climb. I remember nothing of the climb up until I reached her limb, until I began to snake out over the green ice, cooing ludicrously, *Good bird . . . good bird.*

I keep saying "she" and "her" without knowing whether I can tell male from female owls. She looked feminine, at once vulnerable and haughty, a princess in durance.

As I inched out, she leaned back as far as she could get from me, until she must have been teetering on her tailbone. Her struggling had wrapped the wire tight, so no matter how she pulled, her feet remained immovably involved. The yellow eyes opened incredibly wide, in what was inseparably threat and indignation. There was no way to make her understand my intentions.

The great horned owl is a very large bird, a hunter, an exquisitely equipped carnivore, a dismembering machine. Tyrannosaur quickens in her blood. I kept flinching from the stab of the skunk-dispatching beak, which never came. She studied me as I worked the wire free, blinking, raising her wings to let the loops of wire pass under them. I removed my gloves when the work got tighter, though then I had to work faster, too, against the paralyzing cold. When I touched her body with my naked hand, a thrill went through me like an electric shock. I imagined slipping my fingers under her feathers for a moment to warm them, but I never dared.

The loosened wire took a dive onto the ice—baling wire, I figured, trying to imagine how she picked it up. Maybe mousing in a barn. The wire made a musical note when it hit the lake. The owl cocked her head to the sound, but still she had not moved, still she had not realized she was free. I too kept still, imagining a face full of frenzied owl. We stared at each other from the ends of that branch so long that I broke concentration, daydreaming of warmth, began to slip from my handhold. The motion of my grabbing back onto the limb startled her. She flapped. Her eyes announced that she felt nothing hold her down.

Several things happened at once. The owl beat into the air, and though her liftoff was absolutely silent, it startled me so that I lost my grip on the limb, plunging as the owl rose. Between us we achieved a mystical balance, mirror images diverging at equal distances and similar speeds from the same tulip branch. She shot straight up, then veered toward the center of the lake.

I, clearly, never changed direction. Down, down. Down and backwards, with the sky at the same apparent remoteness no matter how far I fell. The tree hadn't seemed so high when I was in it.

If you hit hard enough you actually do see stars. I felt the pain shooting through my bones, savoring it, testing its nuances to see what I had broken. The pain flowed to full tide, then slowly subsided. Nothing had broken, not even the ice. Great was the thanks I gave. I rolled the six or seven feet to shore. As I staggered onto my feet, the owl was beating onward, still visible nearing the far side of the lake, poised to vanish in the owl-colored distance. I stared at her disappearing place until the cold drove me again into motion.

Autumn

T HE FIRST HARD WIND of autumn around the Great
Lakes is called the Witch. The lakemen hate her. She
veers in from the northwest with polar ice bunched at her
breast, whipping barges into harbor, shearing off whitecaps,
beaching everything not anchored down. It's everyone's
bad time. The praying mantis snags a blown leaf with her
saw-tooth arms, bites the pointless gold, swiveling her
head toward starvation. Katydids fall onto the walks, fat
as green cattle, too stunned to move. Tatter-winged moths
cling to screen doors with their last strength. Geese beat
southward from the Great Slave Lake, their gray harp
wings keening in the moonlight.

The princess falls among the dragons.

We are not in our right minds.

Brown leaves flap from the oak branch, crying,
Betrayed!

I climb the hill to do my laundry. Someone left the lights
burning in the laundry room, and the door ajar all night,

and on the walls, moths have gathered by the hundreds, moths of the palest violet, deep purple, purple-brown, white, near-white, gray, chestnut shot with gold, chryso-prase lunas, gigantic polyphemus that would spill over the edge of my hand, all waving and fluttering like leaves in an enchanted forest. A dragonfly angrily circles the light-bulb, like a bombardier whose bomb bays are jammed, and he can neither return nor complete his mission. My im-pulse is to run for my insect guide and identify, identify, identify, but the bounty is too great; I wouldn't know where to begin. I carry some outside in my hands. Those that have the strength flutter vaguely toward the now-greater light of day. Others, falling onto the floor, begin to crawl, some toward the outside, others not, none of them seeming to get very far. As I put my quarters in the wash-ing machine I notice that the jeweled leaves, like the leaves of the forest all around, are falling. Those on the wall still outnumber those on the floor, but the proportion alters moment by moment. This is a moth graveyard. They have come here to die.

Day dawned excessively blue. When I got out of my car, I was singing. I hauled out my blue backpack and arranged its contents on the hood while I sang. A friend says I re-mind him of a Chekhov character, because I sing for no apparent reason, without self-consciousness, as though I were alone. I packed carrots, apples, home-baked bread thick with bran and honey, and, lest I give a too-wholesome impression, two plastic bottles of warm soda. I am prepared for an autumn hike. I have more jackets and sweaters than two people are likely to need, but I don't like the cold. Wool for the outside, bread for the inside, to stoke the fires. I mean to walk on the mountains, and look, and look.

The man in the car parked beside mine had been waiting for who knows what. He seems to take my activity as a signal to get out and rush up the trail before I can get there, while it retains its untrodden purity. I watch him for a time, partially because I come behind and it would have been an effort not to, partially because a red-tailed hawk hovers over his head, moving when he moves, circling when he stops, veering when he veers. The hawk is young, probably this summer's brood, but surely he cannot think of a grown man as prey. I allow myself to think he is playing.

When the man disappears from direct sight, I still know where he is, because of the hawk. It is autumn, and a hawk could see something that size easily moving through the trees. There must be a reason why the hawk wants me to keep an eye on the man, for the hawk's benefit, or the man's, or my own.

I too leave the road to climb the Shut-In trail, stopping at the top of the ridge to eat my carrots. I meant to go the same way as the hawk-man, but he ruined it for me. It's all right. This way turns out better, somehow. A long time passes during which I do, approximately, nothing. I remember this because of the sensation of the near infinite expansion of time, there on the narrow back of the mountain, minute after minute of the changeless pale blue of the sky, the changeless dark grays and black-greens of the forest, the wind that came as a voice high up, scarcely moving the forest as far down as I. I feel like a tree myself, rooted, almost immutable. I cover the carrot butts with leaves, to keep their orange from unbalancing the sleepy earth tones. It must be nearly evening, I think, though the quality of the light has not changed. I return to Sleepy Gap, and, against all odds, enter the clearing at exactly the same moment as the stranger, the hawk man.

I say, "Calling it a day?"

He answers, "I lost my hawk."

He is a beautiful man, compact, with close-cropped silver-black hair and the delicate, pointed face of one who was a fox in a former life. In his left ear lobe shines a golden wire. I note that we are dressed identically, in Levis and denim jackets faded to the color of the winter sky. Our flannel shirts are blue and black plaid, open mid-chest to reveal gray T-shirts. White Reeboks gleam from our feet. Both of us carry pale teal backpacks, though his is slung over his shoulder and mine is still on my back. It looks intentional, as though we were models posing for an outdoor magazine. He doesn't seem to notice the identity of our equipage. He begins to talk, with the urgency of the Ancient Mariner, about hawks, about ospreys, about the trees dying on Mount Mitchell. When he says, "Mount Mitchell," he points to Pisgah, the blue eminence blocking the southern horizon. I wonder if he doesn't know it isn't Mitchell, or is simply indicating the biggest mountain around. The vehemence of his delivery signals to me that these things are not really what's on his mind. They're what you're supposed to say to a stranger at a turnoff on the Blue Ridge Parkway. I wait for him to say what he means. I put on that face you get that says, "You can tell me anything; you'll never see me again." He is quite polite. He stands so that my back can be to the setting sun, which he fights with his hand angled over his eyes.

Finally he says, "The hawk followed me."

"I saw."

"Whenever I tried to climb higher, he screamed and dived at me. He didn't want me to get higher."

"Maybe his nest—" I begin, but it's a false start. There are no nests now.

"No. I think he knows."

"Knows?"

"About me."

I wait for the man to tell me what the hawk might know about him. Though the hawk might know, I don't. The man is very sad. He looks like he's going to weep, and I hope he doesn't, for I would not know what to do.

Uhm . . . what makes you think the hawk . . . ?

But the man is finished with this episode. He gets up and waves to me, starts for his car. I call at his back, "It was nothing. Probably just an accident."

Immediately I wish I hadn't said that. The one sure thing is that there are no accidents. I look over to where the man is sitting in his car. I sense that he is not going to leave until I do, so I climb into mine, turn the key, and drive off, just as the moon heaves over the shoulders of blue Pisgah. The man is still sitting there when I round the curve. Perhaps he never meant to leave at all.

~

What they wanted in the quarry I was never sure. Maybe limestone, or gravel. One could believe that Mordor existed for itself, purposeless and self-begotten, enduring in order to symbolize the desolation of the world. The one sign of life was the house-sized trucks which roared hourly from its gates, laden with—something. The pits were worked by Allied Chemical, which sprawled like a vast crustacean around Syracuse, one claw in the valley, one claw reddening the sky ten miles north at Solvay. Though you knew men must inhabit the yellow cabs of the digging machines, you never saw them. Perhaps it was distance, or the angle of observation from the edge of the pit, but everything exuded soullessness, unpeopled, the kingdom of the automatons.

Used to be that men told stories of wise animals, humans under beast pelts. Now they tell stories of machines that wake one day, thinking and wanting, near-men walking with the buzz of microchips. It is the same story.

Let me admit I loved the quarry.

I make my conservationist friends uneasy because of a romantic attachment to industrial wastelands. Sublime they are, and the more desolate, the more sublime. My first job was with Goodyear Tire in Akron, after the time of its prime, when vast spaces in the old factories stood empty. I was a mailboy, and when I did the factory route, I got so I could finish forty minutes faster than the time allotted. I used those minutes to wander the abandoned plants on Kelly Avenue, miles of them, airy, dusty, pigeon-colonized. One saw foxes, raccoons, dead opossums, which implied living cousins in the rafters. Snakes as thick and dark as tires fattened on the tribes of rats. How these mysterious slithering monsters got there through the whole body of the city must be wonderful to tell. Brass-knuckled ailanthus pounded between bricks, buckled skylights. Day filtered through chinks in the ceilings and fissures in the walls with a soft, buttery radiance, not unlike—if one narrowed one's eyes so only the light was visible—the pale diffusion in the forest in earliest spring. The crumbling factories possessed some qualities of beauty denied to the flowering wood. Defeat. Desperation. Hard use followed by abandonment, like the men who had hammered their lives away there and lay now under the headstones of North Hill.

One breathed an air of danger, imagined and actual. If *you* had found a way into this desolation, what else might have? To one who grew up with Saturday matinee vampires and walking mummies, each dark staircase provided a fresh test of grit. Besides, whatever it might be doing for one's soul, wandering about in the old plants *looked* like goofing off, and we mailboys were salaried, and the union workers were ever vigilant to find us in a trespass, report us to the supervisor. Most of the mailboys goofed off in plain sight, near the lobby vending machines, where one could get bars of white candy surrounding centers of whipped blond chocolate as subtle as air. They would be caught, reported, switched to a route that provided more constant scrutiny. Not me. Never caught. Never visible. I wandered among gleaming-eyed creatures, hidden in wilderness as surely as if I'd taken to the Amazon. I did the factory route so well and so happily that they switched me to the fifth floor, where the president and the chairman of the board presided over phalanxes of plutocrats, and they called it a promotion.

Anyway, between the Allied quarry and the neighborhoods of Syracuse lay Skytop Landfill, which I loved even better, as one loves wrecks that manage nevertheless a wild and forlorn beauty. The landfill lay within comfortable jogging distance, and one ran there in all weather, except the bitterest cold, to see what treasures may have been abandoned, what creature may have found a temporary home.

Landfill wildlife was surprisingly diverse. Deer, raccoon, rat, opossum, weasels—one, perhaps, expects these. But to ponds made out of the wheel ruts of heavy machinery came in spring mallards, raising whole broods until new dumping erased their homes, new dumping accompanied by new ruts which would be the next year's wetlands. Pheasants exploded from cover in that coronary-inducing way they have. Herons stalked the wheel ruts, brazen and heedless as tourists. In the farthest, deepest pond—one that may have been in fact natural—lived a family of muskrats. Overhead on summer evenings kestrels soared and twittered, taking advantage of the openness of the place, the bare acres scattered with scrub, shining with glass and furniture and defunct appliances. Sandpipers and the occasional coot bobbed in filthy waters. Wonders might fly up at your feet.

The indwelling spirit of Skytop Landfill took the shape of killdeer. Spring came when the killdeer came, crying plaintively from the March hills. The call is wild and sad, a lamentation. If you follow one, the bird recedes, still crying from her broken heart. Nothing you can do will heal it. She won't let you close enough to try. You know it is partially a sham—nobody is that sad that long—but you fall for it, because it changes a squalid dump into an opera of inclemency.

South of the landfill grew a fringe of trees. Beyond the trees stretched the quarries.

The quarries consisted of two pits, one long-ago abandoned and filled with emerald water. When whatever commodity they dug became profitable again, they opened a new hole, wider, more efficiently dug, though perhaps I should substitute "daringly" for "efficiently." Each season the workers in the new pit pared closer to the old pit wall, until the green lake lay, soup in a porcelain bowl, enclosed by a curve of soil that I could stretch my body across. It was too reckless. People wouldn't do that. Machines did it, having no conception of mortality. The damp cliff face should have told them. Leakage in a tangled rope of extruded water should have thundered, *Too close.*

One day the narrow wall could take no more. The rim gave. Green water fell four days and nights. I saw it at night, when it was like a black table tilted, smooth and agleam in the starlight. Had anyone lived in the river valley, they would have been washed away. As it was, the furnaces of the much-argued-over municipal trash burner went out; the goliath chemical trucks had to detour through the city, where people sent up a great shout, supposing they had sprung up overnight with their dust and din. Expatriated mallards circled a few times, flew on. In mallard memory, lakes must come and go. The moon leaned over, vainly looking for her image where the water had been.

Plants should have taken over the drying lake bottom more quickly than they did. Mullein was the first volunteer. It found ooze, but little soil. Summer withered everything without some depth of root. Charms of finches forayed into the gap, found nothing, homed to the rich thistles of the rim. You could walk on the dry lake with impunity. It was dry and bare. It was too high for the machines in the working pit to see you. Fish bones bleached between the rocks. A year before, ninety feet of water would have stood over your head. The rusty gleam in the mud after rain was rusty tools pounded free by the downpour. There were the hulks of a few old cars, that you never looked inside of, for fear there would be bones.

The cold hit early that fall. When hunting season opened, an ice roof had already formed over the smaller ponds, gray-white and as brittle as eggshell. I walked the dry lake then. On that day there were hunters, many, or a few firing with maniacal frequency. Red and yellow shell casings shone in the frosty grass. Surrounded by a mile of open ground on all sides, I didn't fear being mistaken for a deer. But why I'd gone there at all I couldn't say. I had work to do. It was cold, gray, barren, and the rifle shots bore the timbre of empty irritability.

Then I saw a shape coming toward me, a raccoon, maybe frightened out of the woods by the gunfire. It broke through the eggshell ice on the puddles as it came, a noisy and awkward thing for a wild animal to do. It dragged something behind it. A shadow followed it across the ground. It kept coming at me, right for me, as though it wanted something. Maybe it didn't see me. I moved so it would see me. It stopped, turned wearily away, as though deflected by habit rather than genuine caution. I saw then what it dragged behind it. Its backside and one hind leg had been sheared away by bullets. Its organs hung in the air like jumbled flowers, beautiful and oddly bloodless. Death glazed its eyes, even though it kept moving.

The guns began again, farther off, by the valley road.

I should mention that informed views of nature are uniformly bloody.

I should mention that there is a bug on Java, *Ptilocerus,* which wears under its abdomen a clump of bright hairs that marks a gland which secretes a substance irresistible to ants. As the ants feed, they gradually fathom that the secretion is a narcotic, and as paralysis chills their limbs, their "benefactor" pierces their chitin and commences to suck them dry. Those who have seen it call *Ptilocerus* profoundly beautiful.

Traveling Companion

I WANT TO KNOW whether animals have religion. Certainly they do, in the sense that they desire some things and dread others without understanding them, but that is religion pretty low down. I want to know if there is a sense of aspiration, of thankfulness. Triceratops could look up at the stars. Did he? If so, what did he think? Surely in some dim and vague way he must have thought *something*. Were they the twinkling eyes of a great herd which, curiously, did not respond no matter how one roared and stamped? What of *Australopithecus,* lying on his back in the Great Rift Valley, chewing a stalk of grass, gazing through the clear air at the Void? Did he see the campfires of people who managed somehow to lift themselves up above the leopards and whirlwinds? What of Neanderthal, who buried his dead with such tenderness we know he already conceived for himself a soul?

The first time somebody showed me the moons of Jupiter and the rings of Saturn—all in one night—in a backyard scope, I fell into a swoon as surely as Galileo's countrymen when he showed them the imperfect visage of the sun. It's not that I doubted they were there, but only that I would ever be vouchsafed the blessing of seeing them. To hear of some great prodigy allows for the mind to run on merrily in its accustomed slot, but actually to *see* the thing requires reconfigurations, journeys, interior tempests. Back in high school I saw an instructional movie that made the point that the same level of magnification that would reveal a hydrogen atom in my hand, would make visible quasars on the edge of the universe. Did it *mean* such a thing? Did it mean to imply I stand at the pivot of two echoing immensities, and if so, what in the cosmos should be my response?

In his book *Red Giants and White Dwarfs,* Robert Jastrow, director of the Goddard Institute for Space Studies, parses the immensities with a chain of analogies. If the Astrodome were an atom, the nucleus, the actual solid matter of it, would be a Ping-Pong ball in the center. The relation of the sun to the orbit of Pluto preserves roughly the same proportion. If all the stars of the Milky Way were oranges, the galaxy would *still* have a diameter of 20 million miles. And if Shakespeare and Plato were oak trees, I would be a violet, amazed and self-concealing, between their curling toes. But really, such information is valuable even if difficult to put to immediate use. It instills a sense of proportion; like the first glimpse of the white sails of Captain Cook appearing, as if through the power of the gods, in a Polynesian harbor, it brings the message that we are not alone, and that we should consider simultaneously the postures of defense and elation.

I love antique astronomical chronicles for their sweet faith in the providence behind creation, for their emphasis on a uniformity and invariability in the cosmos, which is actually nowhere to be found. At a certain point in the history of philosophy, some Greek or other decided that stasis was to be preferred over change, that matter, given its head, would be at rest. This does not seem to me to be particularly *attractive,* much less true. Keep the news from Newton, but the universe brims with lovely eccentricities. Our homely sun wobbles and roars and breaks out in spots like an adolescent and hurls out fiery prominences a hundred times the size of Earth. Beyond the solar system lie Cepheid variables, yellow supergiants, that vary as a uniform individual rate, altering their brightness by as little as ten or as much as seven hundred percent. Mingled with them are the Mira variables, which shed luminous matter around themselves as a burning veil, then draw it back in a closed system of ejection and absorption. Some astronomers assert that all interstellar dust at one time passed through the red crucible of a Mira variable. The name comes from the star Omicron Ceti, nicknamed Mira, "the wonderful." This process would be wonderful enough, but, as usual, there is the matter of size to consider. Most Mira variables are gigantic even by cosmic standards. Mira herself, in the position of our sun, would extend beyond the orbit of Mars.

Not yet to mention the cataclysmic variables, the novae. Once every human generation or so, a giant explodes in our star system. Once every two or three centuries, one explodes close enough to be marked by the naked eye at high noon. During its brief glory, a novae outshines a thousand million ordinary stars, and radiates as much energy as our sun has burned in the last half billion years. What remains where the nova was is a neutron star with a core so dense that a cubic centimeter of it weighs a billion tons. (Note: How does one weigh something that weighs a billion tons? A Ripley's book of records my college roommate had asserted that the Great Galaxy of Andromeda weighs twelve thousand duodecillion long tons. It's not that I doubt it; it's that I want to know how such a thing is known.) If the neutron core is very, very large, approaching three solar masses, the collapse of the nova-remnant continues until it forms a black hole, absolute material zero—no, worse than that, a material negative, a negation, a hole in the continuum. Theoretically there is no downward limit on the size of a black hole. A star with the mass of a thousand trillion tons can shrink to the size of a jelly bean, a dime, a microbe. Matter in infinite compression. How many black holes can dance on the head of a pin? "But," Jastrow points out, "intuition tells us that such an object cannot exist"—intuition, or blind terror, a sort of disgust with the excesses of speculation. Something so far in violation of human proportion *should* be unthinkable.

Actually, having analyzed Jastrow's statement, I find that intuition tells me no such thing. In my brain there is a whole file for, "Things That Don't Make Sense Unless You Get Out of Your Ordinary Mind-Set," an activity at which I'm pretty good. Wouldn't an infinitesimal black hole in the brains of some people explain a lot? Wouldn't it serve as a tiny door between worlds, helping to justify vision, strokes of genius, bouts of apparent madness?

How many of the objects lost from your life might *really* have fallen into a black hole, a happenstance for which no one, after all, bears responsibility?

━━━

Thomas Chalmers, a Scottish polymath, in the first decade of the nineteenth century began in Glasgow a series of weekday lectures, designed partially to help businessmen incorporate Christianity into their daily dealings, and partially to reconcile science and religion. "Reconciliation" came from Chalmers chiefly in the form of repeated instances of human smallness in the face of the immensity of creation. In 1817 Chalmers published "The Christian Revelation Viewed in Connexion with the Modern Astronomy," which contained the following prophecy:

> In all these greater arrangements of divine wisdom, we can see that God has done the same things [light, heat, seasons] for the accommodation of the planets as he has done for the earth we inhabit. And shall we say, that the resemblance stops here, because we are not in a situation to observe it? Shall we say, that this scene of magnificence has been called into being merely for the amusement of a few astronomers? Shall we measure the counsels of heaven by the narrow impotence of the human faculties? or conceive that silence and solitude reign throughout the mighty empire of nature . . . that not a worshiper of the Divinity is to be found through the wide extent of yon vast and immeasurable regions?

People have always suspected that the stars and themselves have something important to do with each other. Mostly it was a one-way relationship; the stars looked down, affecting or controlling human destiny without being affected in return. Early in the Enlightenment, the possibilities for relationship were aborted by the assumption that stars were a stupendously extended litter of dead lights, mindless worlds, uninhabited and without moral consequence, shavings off the worktable of the clockmaker God. On Chalmers and his like, however—despite the dewy enthusiasm of their prose—it dawned that the ancients might not have been such fools after all, that it was actually rather unscientific to think of ourselves and our world as an exception and an anomaly, that if our sun is a star and the other stars be suns, why shouldn't there be planets revolving around them, sprung from the same Creator and therefore equally rife with happy voices singing praises? In Chalmers's essay, the homocentrism of the Middle Ages vanishes like morning mist. Here a nineteenth-century Carl Sagan speculates on the billions and billions of prayers lifted up from the devout hearts— or whatevers—of the cosmos. The style is precious, but the sentiment is not. We, thinking scientific speculation is an advance over piety, imagine the sophisticated races of the stars broadcasting electronic messages, laying scientific traps among the stars to catch their peers. Chalmers, thinking that faith was highest, does the aliens the courtesy of imagining them at prayer. The cosmos do not change. We do.

For all his variegated optimism, Chalmers does not

foresee a meeting among these scattered brethren. It must
be sufficient to perceive and praise.

> Who shall assign a limit to the discoveries of future
> ages? Who can prescribe to science her boundaries,
> or restrain the active and insatiable curiosity of man
> within the present circle of his acquirements? We
> may guess with plausibility what we cannot anticipate
> with confidence. The day may yet be coming when
> our instruments of observation shall be inconceivably
> more powerful. They may ascertain still more decisive
> points of resemblance. . . . Perhaps some large city,
> the vast metropolis of a mighty empire, may expand
> into a visible spot by the powers of some future
> telescope. . . . There is no end to this conjecture,
> and to the men of other times we leave the full assur-
> ance . . . that yon planetary orbs are so many worlds,
> that they teem with life, and that the mighty Being
> who presides in high authority over this scene of
> grandeur and astonishment, has there planted the
> worshipers of his glory.

Go to contemporary physics to find the vocabulary
of rapture standing so bare and unashamed. I myself long
achingly for the opportunity to employ the phrase, "yon
planetary orbs." The sentiment, however, you find everywhere, from vanguard physicists to the fantastical housewives whose sagas of ravishment by extraterrestrials
empurple the pages of the supermarket tabloids. My guess
is that Chalmers would not be so much astonished by space
travel as he would think it a perilous and unnecessary

confirmation of what the eye can see quite well, and that heart knew before it saw. Out there dwells the Magnificence.

∾

I was born into the last generation that knew a time before space travel, that will never be able to think of space travel as routine. Our fathers started it. We continued it, but it will mostly be our children, our grandchildren, hurling themselves into Chalmers's singing immensities. To no succeeding generation will it ever again seem so wondrous, so unlooked-for. No one after us will be able to look at pictures of the moon and claim that they were taken in a studio.

I remember clearly the Night of the Satellite. It was the first time in my life when events made a difference, the first time I recognized my involvement in matters beyond the few backyards and the handful of playmates that formed my world. Someone said, "You will remember this day for the rest of your life," and I knew it was right. There would be no shrugging this off as one of those phantasms adults always wanted you to feel were significant but about which you couldn't care less. It *was* significant. It was the door open into the coming world, and not my father nor my mother, nor any of the giants looming above my play, could enter so thoroughly as I.

My best pal then was Ronnie Evans. He was two years older than I, but had failed back to the same grade. I spent hours waiting for him to get out of summer reading class so we could be about the serious business of vacation. I'm trying to remember if I liked Ronnie all that much. Not that it mattered; one's friend was one's friend, and, as in conditions of barbarism and chivalry, one had certain rights and duties regardless of the presence of genuine affection. Ronnie was too slow for there to be much actual sympathy between us. But he was rough-hewn and outdoorsy, and oblivious to the sorts of distinctions with which I was burdened. He had no ponderable imagination, which made him a perfect playground for mine. Perhaps it's enough to say that he was the first friend I had to whom I was utterly unsuited, so that we had to learn from each other before we could communicate at all. The value of such forced accommodation cannot be overestimated.

Plus, Ronnie was kindhearted. This quality fascinated me. I was not particularly notable for it, and what portion of it I eventually acquired had to be learned. His was natural, unconscious, unwearying. I could take advantage of it, of course, but I could also sample and mimic it. It was the same thing he had that I needed.

The heat of our friendship lasted maybe two years. When our relationship ended, it had less to do with us than with revolution in the external world, an upheaval that changed alliances among boys and made adults reconsider the courses of their lives. One could look up the exact date, but one would rather remember the *feel* of it, like the first day of school, when sensation is new and sharp and the way stands open on infinite possibility.

We had spent that day hiking. Ronnie, uncharacteristically, had been telling jokes, a few of which I still remember. This disturbed me a little, for I had always been the joke teller. I liked Ronnie that day, maybe because of the jokes, for the first time seeing him as more than a co-star in my personal adventure serial. Generally he earned my admiration for things like remembering to bring matches so we could burn debris at a favorite campsite, or for making a whistle of a blade of grass. We spent hours with one foot on either side of the little creek, overturning rocks to find crayfish and nymphs beneath. We called this "fishing," though fish were the things we saw least often. I don't know whether it would have occurred to me to invade the natural world at all without Ronnie. Perhaps I would have just stuck to my books. Together, we were something. I was a naturalist and he a hunter, potentially a great team, even if the potential would not be realized.

That was the day, too, when I first noticed us talking at cross-purposes. I spoke of dinosaurs and of space travel. I longed to be forever at the creek, levering stones, curious, delighted, unchangeably a child. Ronnie's face had begun to scar with acne. He talked of forming a rock-and-roll band, suggesting "the Youngbloods" and "the Whirlwinds" as possible names. I knew enough about rock and roll to point out that he didn't play an instrument, and my elementary school violin would probably not do. I liked "the Whirlwinds" better for a name, but I really didn't like the band idea at all. Ronnie was talking about something he knew more about than I, and that was disturbing, new. He had stopped listening to me. Heretofore I had been the talker and he the listener. But that day he talked, not stupidly either, and I stared into the shiver of dry leaves.

Dusk deepened as we sat at our campsite, burning grass and twigs in a desultory way. We had little to say to each other. His hormones and my imagination raged, and there was no room even in our loose confederation for all of that. Still, neither of us was in a hurry to leave. We waited for something to happen to make it all right again.

A voice began shouting Ronnie's name. It was his father's, a voice I don't remember hearing more than a few times, and rare enough even for Ronnie that he jumped and ran. I followed, with the urgency of one not anxious to be left in a strange woods at nightfall. It was a strong voice coming from a great distance, and we were afraid.

When we ran into the Evans's street, I saw my father's car. My mother stood beside it, with my infant sister in her arms. It should have been a reassuring sight, but something in the strangeness of it, the unexpectedness, put me off. I looked hard at the faces as I ran, trying to read if I were in trouble or there had been a catastrophe. Everyone was smiling. That in itself was not reassuring, for even a child recognizes smiles that do not express pleasure.

Mother said, "We came early to take you home. We wanted to see it together."

It sounded like she meant my sister, but I had already seen her. I said, "What?"

Mother looked into the air, unable to point with my sister in her arms. I looked where she looked. There, moving perceptibly, like a shooting star of miraculous durability, was a fire in the sky. Red, I remember it, though I remember the whole sky that night as a spilled burgundy flecked with rubies.

"*Sputnik,*" my father said, "the first space ship."

Ronnie said, "Traveling Companion. It means 'Traveling Companion.'"

He said that without looking up. He was already feeding the cats, whom he called with a long melisma made of their names—*Here scoots-a-boots-a-blackie.* I thought he might at least like to see it, but he went on feeding the cats with his meticulous single-mindedness, refusing to look. That was the sort of thing he did when he didn't want to do what I wanted to do, but had no better suggestion of his own. It made me angry that time, as it never had before. I turned away, vowing never to speak to him unless spoken to first.

Mrs. Evans had my gear ready to go home. I felt there was something more to my early departure than just *Sputnik,* a quarrel among the adults, a mishap, but no one mentioned anything else. In the car my mother sat with her head sticking through the window, so she could watch the red streak sinking into the trees. It was she who said, "You will remember this day for the rest of your life."

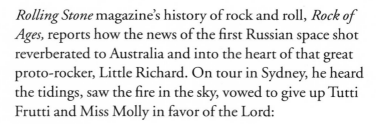

Rolling Stone magazine's history of rock and roll, *Rock of Ages,* reports how the news of the first Russian space shot reverberated to Australia and into the heart of that great proto-rocker, Little Richard. On tour in Sydney, he heard the tidings, saw the fire in the sky, vowed to give up Tutti Frutti and Miss Molly in favor of the Lord:

> That night Russia sent off that very first *Sputnik.* It looked as though the big ball of fire came directly over the stadium about two or three hundred feet above our heads. It shook my mind. I got up from the piano and said, "This is it. I am through. I am leaving show business to go back to God."

In 1781, Sir William Herschel became the first man in modern history to discover a planet, frigid Uranus. Six years later his watchfulness added two moons to that distant world, Titania and Oberon. The moons' names are anomalous, in having nothing to do with classical mythology, but rather being the names of Shakespearian fairies. They must have had some relevance to that blue world that escapes me as I write. One associates Titania and Oberon with a midsummer revel in a magic wood, whereas there is nothing summery about that ball of frozen gas, beautiful as it is from a distance. Herschel's sister, Caroline, an astronomer in her own right, discovered three nebulae and eight comets. His son, Sir John Herschel, thus born into a family versed in wonders, published in 1833 a book called *Treatise on Astronomy,* which warns against misinterpretation and "vulgar errors" arising from imperfect apprehension or bad observational habits. He admonishes the apprentice scientist:

> He must loosen his hold on all crude and hastily adopted notions, and must strengthen himself . . . for the unprejudiced admission of any conclusion which shall appear to be supported by careful observation and logical argument, even if it should prove of a nature adverse to notions he may have previously formed for himself, or taken up, without examination, on the credit of others. . . . We must purge our sight before we can receive and contemplate as they are the lineaments of truth and nature.

The purging of sight is the hardest and yet, ultimately, most rewarding exercise the watcher of the world may undertake. It is the hyssop and scouring rush of philosophy, for if everything were the way you first thought it was, what a small and grievous existence you would have, in a mean little cosmos whose every action followed the least and hastiest of mortal plans. What a blessing to be wrong in one's first impressions! The initiate sees gigantic forms of greater truth hidden behind the apparent details of reality, rather as a mariner sees a mountain of ice under the little dome that breaks the surface. The worst mistake a scientist—or a poet—can make is ever to accept the least common denominator as an image of truth. Herschel speaks of the initiate:

> The planets, which appear only as stars somewhat brighter than the rest, are to him spacious, elaborate, and habitable worlds, several of them much greater and far more curiously furnished than the earth he inhabits . . . and the stars themselves . . . which to ordinary apprehension present only lucid sparks or brilliant atoms, are to him suns of various and transcendent glory—effulgent centres of life to myriads of unseen worlds.

> Complete knowledge brings delight. This is a truth generally forgotten because partial knowledge brings, generally, misery.

⚋

Summer night. Low music from the dormitory windows. Perfumes rise when feet drag across the shimmering grass. I'm part of the faculty at a summer school session on—

how eerily Chalmers-like—the integration of business
and the humanities. Our final session ends triumphantly,
and partying extends to midnight, everyone happy with
one another and the progress everyone has made toward
harmonizing these mutually repellent principles. Someone sets up a telescope on the wet lawn. It takes me a
while to figure out how to look into the thing, but when
I finally do, successfully, what I see is not what I expected.
Carol, my friend guiding me through the process whis-
pers, "That is the ecliptic." I expected dust and smudge.
What I find this "ecliptic" to be is great smoking hearths,
splendor, vacancy, magnetic seas enveloping worlds of ice,
continents racing across gulfs of fire, crystal mountains
ten miles high, bottomless valleys, deeps and immensities.
The scent of the crushed grass massages the only sense left
out of the glory visible through the lens. When my turn
is finished, I pass the scope on to the next looker. I leave
the party. I return to my room. I am deeply melancholy.
I cannot figure out why, until I stop for a moment and analyze the feeling. It is something, after all, quite precise.

It is homesickness.

Curlews

WE ARE IMMORTAL until the hour death first seizes our imagination. This goes for species as well as individuals. To die requires that you must have, at least once, considered death and thought of it as beautiful. All spiritual advances are advances in aesthetics.

The cockroach, the horseshoe crab, the lungfish have never quite come to grips.

～～

Easter that year was as early as it can be. Wind blustered from the flatlands by Lake Erie, blowing the tan dust of winter's end into nostrils and eyes. There were, of course, no flowers except for what the deacons brought from the florist shop on Pioneer Street. Dust scoured a flowerless, flat, yellow land, all under a dry gold light that rubbed even the dust and the barrenness to ringing clean. Emmanuel Church was not beautiful so much as lively and expectant, its walls stark with store-bought lilies. The men still wore their black winter suits, their tight smiles expressing Dutch Reformed abashment before an indecorous feast, neither Protestant nor Northern. Only the boy's mother wore anything like an Easter bonnet, because he begged her to, a low pink dome surmounted by a corona of pale flowers and small, hard fruits. It didn't matter that she removed it the minute she entered the building; the boy was satisfied.

The boy knew how things were meant to be, even if he'd never seen them that way himself. He read everything. He listened to adult conversation with reptilian concentration. He knew when adults were wrong, and also that to be told they were wrong irritated them so much it was really not worth the effort. He knew that Easter Sunday required bright bonnets of the women. He knew that he himself should have a new suit, and that it should be a gay color like green or cream, though his indifference to his own clothing allowed that to pass by. He knew that there should be flowers, certainly more flowers than there were, not only from the florist, but covering the hills and meadows, covering the world in commemoration of the miracle.

Nothing was right. Though he had no proof, he suspected that his church had picked the wrong date for Easter—deliberately, out of an unaccountable impulse to ruin. He remembered three or four Easters, and there were never enough flowers, not real ones, from the ground. The lilies were too unreal to count. They might have been manufactured, for all their snowy perfection. What there was, was sleet, cold, nothing pertinent to Resurrection but the blazing acid light.

Easter meant Jesus had been dead three days. He had risen and was alive in heaven. The boy made sure of the mathematical points, asking repeatedly, "And that means that after three days Jesus rose from the dead, and *that* means that after three days *we* rise from the dead? Each time they answered him, *yes*.

Much of the world was so mysterious that there was no way of telling what was really a mystery and what was being obscured by the people from whom answers had to be extracted. When he could, the boy found out things on his own. When he couldn't, as a final recourse, he asked adults, never quite trusting the answers, but hoping at least for a clue to send him to the right place from which to continue on his own.

Three days, though: that seemed doubtful, or at least incomplete. Adults were always leaving things out of their explanations, sometimes because they didn't know better, sometimes because they didn't realize he truly needed answers to the questions he asked. So if he asked again and again about the three days, it was because he needed to know, and again and again they told him that's how it was, that's what Easter stood for.

"Does this have to begin on Good Friday and end on Easter, or can it be any Friday and any Sunday, or can it be any three days at all?"

They said it could be any three days at all. This news sat and brooded in his heart. The reason he kept asking was the body in the field on Good Friday.

The boy's father had taken him kite flying. There was something wrong in this, on Good Friday and all. He wanted to sit and think about death and Jesus, not out of morbidity, really, but because there was something to be obtained in the world, something fine and beyond his ordinary reach, by observation of the right ceremony at the right time, by even knowing what the right ceremony was. In a book a saint had done certain things, and God put blood on his hands and feet, and this was meant to be wonderful. There were things you were supposed to do just before Easter—kite flying was not one of them—and if you did them, you might get in a book, or at least boring and stupid people would stop thinking of you as one of *them*. Nothing could be said. He already knew what could and couldn't be expressed to adults, what they would accept, what would frighten them and make them force on you the opposite of what you asked.

His father seemed certain that it was kite-flying weather. The light came cold and dry and golden, the kite-upholder, so perhaps he was right, perhaps this too was a ceremony, and his father knew more than he thought. He said yes to a kite, picturing a plain white one, unfigured, a holy blankness. His father brought home a red one, with a print of fighter planes with teeth at the front like tigers, and the name in shivering yellow letters, "Flying Tigers."

They drove to the open field across from the city park, where there was a great water tower that sang if you hit it with a stick, thirty acres free of wires and trees. Other kites were aloft already, many of them, and the boy thrilled that his father had been right about this, that it truly was kite-flying weather. There was plenty of room in the sky, despite the blue kites, red, yellow, box kites like the stuffed, bright-colored garbage bags that blow around the streets on windy nights. Not one was white; his father had been right again.

As soon as he got out of the car, the boy saw the puppy in the ditch at the roadside. His father told him to get away from it, handing him the kite.

"What killed it?"

The puppy didn't look smashed, but his father thought it must have been a car anyway. He said, "Come on, get away from there."

"How long has it been dead?"

"Not long . . . of course it's been cold enough—now get away, we're not here for that. You know you have to run in order to get the kite into the air."

The boy did know a few things and resented being told the ones he knew. His father wanted him to forget the puppy lying dead at the roadside, and the very urgency of his father's attitude made him suspicious. Was this one of those mysteries he had come upon prematurely, that made everybody purse their lips and say, "You're too young for that now"? But he knew he could not push his father much further now; if he wanted to know more, he would have to ask later, when he could make it look like a random thought rather than the obsession it was becoming. For the rest of the afternoon, his father must not suspect he was thinking of the corpse.

The body was gold with the same gold as the light and the sifting dust. He wanted to scrape it once with the toe of his shoe to see if gold was the puppy's color, or the dust that settled everywhere, invisible until it came to the ground, swirling in little cyclones over the dry grass. But the boy ran as he was told, playing string out behind until the tiger kite leapt into the air.

When he'd asked how long the dog had been dead, his father had answered, "Not long." How long was that? Hours? Days? Two days? One? If the puppy had died today, that would mean it would be dead three days on Easter Sunday, an exact match, no dickering, no rabbinical

questions, just and wholly like Jesus. The boy knew that
if he came back to this spot in three days he would see the
puppy rise from the dead. Faith settled like a pale crown
over his head. There was no possibility of doubt. When
he came back to this spot, the puppy would be watching
him from heaven, and everything would be confirmed.

The next morning he went with his mother to the
supermarket, because he knew she would pass the kite
field, and she would stop and let him look if he said he had
lost something. She did stop, but far from the puppy, so
the boy had to run along the field's edge, pretending to
search for something the location of which he knew exactly.
It lay where it had lain before, its belly swollen, flies clustered on its exposed eye. He didn't slap the flies away; anything may be part of the miracle.

He asked his mother, "When Jesus rises on the third
day, is it right at the beginning of the day, right at dawn?"

She told him, "Yes."

He'd come to the field Sunday, if he had to walk, if he
had to lie about why, and the puppy would be gone.

So Easter that year was as early as it could be, dry, cold,
the air brilliant with emptiness. The men stood at the
church door with their cigarettes, the thin hair blowing
backwards from their heads. The boy sensed that they
didn't altogether like a day to make its own rules, to com-
plicate a matter otherwise as predictable and steadfast as
death. But during the service they had at least to mention
it was Easter, had to admit this one miraculous day in the
dreary year. The boy felt a shared secret between himself
and God. One day when they told him he was too young
to worry about such things, he would turn from them and
answer, *It's all right; I already know.*

The boy considered not going to the field to look at all. It was possible a sanitation truck had picked the body up, in which case the puppy would rise from the bed of the sanitation truck, or from the silvery detritus of the landfill. Faith glittered in the center of his brain like a yellow jewel, like a saint in a book, but better, somehow, because bloodless, secret. Only uncertainty about what would manifest faith more fully led him to ask to go kite flying that afternoon. He didn't need proof, but he had begun to think he was meant to bear witness—not to prophesy, exactly, but, if asked, to answer, *I have seen it with my own eyes.*

The wind that bore the kites up on Good Friday had never stopped, and on the horizon they could make out kites already soaring over the golden field. His father had been surprised by the request, considering the boy's earlier reluctance, but had been glad, too, and talked more than usual on the way to the field, the Easter ham and spiced apples glowing in their bellies. The boy was not listening. He was thinking about standing at the spot where the puppy had been, where the people might see him bear witness or not, but he would *know.*

They parked near enough to where they had parked before that the boy, though he meant to delay and savor the discovery, almost immediately caught the puppy in the corner of his eye. By running very fast away from the site, he was able to convince himself that he had seen nothing, or if he had, that it was a temptation to unbelief and not the vacant roadside that must *really* be there. Closer and closer back the boy circled, with the kite string jerking in his hand, longing to pull into the updraft. The flatness of the field was such that, even far off, he could not avoid seeing the puppy. Finally he ran to its side, not looking at

it directly, for then his father would know why he really
had wanted to come to the field. The swelling in its belly
had deflated, and a few thin bones shone through the
melting pelt. The eyes were eaten away. It was dead, just
plain dead, dead forever. It had not risen with the Lord
on Easter morning.

His father was looking, so he ran into the center of the
field, trying at once to think about the puppy and not
tangle the others' strings. The kite wanted to go high, and
he kept playing out string. He thought it might be the
highest kite in the field, but that too might be a decep-
tion, a simple trick effected by God, that most devious of
grown-ups. Even when his father was calling him, he ran
a little farther, to the fence that was the field's end. The
wind never wavered, gold, bright, cold, always the fine gold
dust ready to be tasted if he opened his mouth. The boy
was crying. He had not felt sorry for the puppy until that
moment, sorry for its being so dead and fly-blown under
the yellow dust. He knew he must run back toward his
father at last, reeling in string so they could go home.

Pigs, rats, goats, cats introduced into a previously isolated
ecosystem can cause environmental disaster. Many indige-
nous Polynesian species are either extinct or threatened beyond reasonable hope of recovery. The brown tree snake,
probably a stowaway on American aircraft landing from
New Guinea in World War II, has decimated bird life on
the island of Guam. The amazing thing is that it takes so
little to change so much. A shotgun blast. The draining of

a single pond. It is infuriating that one's soul, one's sense of responsibility, must be engaged every second.

In uninhabited areas, wildlife is often tame and unafraid. Guns are not necessary. The creatures walk into your hands.

On one island an entire species of bird was wiped out in a few years by a lighthouse keeper's cat.

After recovering from near-extinction by the fur trade, the sea otter finds itself threatened again by fishermen who blame it for a dramatic decrease in the abalone harvest. Though proof exists that the abalone beds were decimated by silt from the construction of the Pacific Coast Highway, the sight of another mammal with a salable commodity in its paws drives us wild.

Whole genera of large mammals disappeared from the Americas within a few thousand years of mankind's appearance. Few sane biologists or anthropologists believe these events were unrelated.

The American Army gave Plains Indians blankets taken from smallpox wards. Smallpox, an Old World disease, went through the native population like wildfire.

In pioneer Ohio, especially around Hinckley and in the Western Reserve, a series of stupendous hunts was organized to clear the area of "dangerous" animals. Hundreds of men formed a circle in the forest and drove the game to a cleared space in the center, where others of our kind stood with loaded rifles. One hunt in Freedom, Ohio, in 1818, bagged twenty bears, eleven wolves, seven hundred deer, an incalculable measure of wild turkeys and assorted game. The bounty of the land was so great that it could support this sport for several years.

In the 1850s, British authorities detoured shipments of food away from the starving Irish on the grounds that charity would encourage dissolute ways. On the west coast of Ireland, in the Cliffs of Moher, nests the kittiwake, a gull with an especially piercing, disturbing cry. The legend grew that the kittiwake learned its cry from starving people who, in desperation, climbed the cliffs looking for birds' eggs, and fell screaming into the sea below.

Half of all species of plants and animals on dry land inhabit the tropical rain forests. This stupefying diversity arises, probably, from the fact that the tropics have been tropics for a very long time. While glaciers marched over the roof and floor of the world, and oceans invaded and retreated in response to the ice's moods, the tropics sat relatively untouched, multiplying their grandeur and abundance. Besides, it is in the nature of a tropical ecosystem to be diverse, even as it is in the far north for there to be a greater number of individuals of fewer species: twenty kinds of, say, bee-eater in an acre of Hawaiian forest, twenty million bison on the Great Plains. Every square inch in the rain forest is a garden.

Since World War II half the tropical forests of the world have disappeared. Those that remain dwindle hourly. Some are cleared for highways or farms. More are cleared to raise cattle. Most are ground into pulpwood, a unique biota transformed into used-car ads in the morning paper. As a generation, we preside over the mass extermination of half the known species of the world—God knows how many unknown—a holocaust, counting the great Pleistocene die-off as part of our achievement, unparalleled since the cancellation of the dinosaurs.

Students are generally good at getting to the sour
contradictions of an issue, even if sometimes only half-
intentionally, having intended at the moment merely to
irritate the certainty of their instructor. Presenting this
scenario in a humanities class, I was confronted by a mis-
chievous look and a waving hand, which, when called
upon, asked, "So what?" The student had a grasp of how
things look like they work. He pointed out that the earth
bounces—or has bounced—back from everything Chaos
has been able to throw at her, that our going on about rhi-
nos or whales or the Wide Open Spaces is basically sentimental, that some of the places we prize most—Ireland, the
Scottish Highlands, Manhattan, the Cote d'Azur—are,
ecologically speaking, hell. The most beautiful creatures
in the world could disappear without affecting us all that
much, and should their disappearance have an effect un-
foreseen, should we quickly follow them to oblivion, again,
so what? It's not as though we are going to last forever anyway. Nothing, especially something as big and complicated as a mammal, does.

On the level of logic, the statement is unanswerable.
Some people, however, mistake the "logical" view for the
scientific one, so it needs to be pointed out that logic is a
technique and not a philosophy, a checklist and not a program, and that, once certain basic premises are accepted,
logic can be used to support the most absurd and ghastly
things. Science is a form of philosophy that generally de-
emphasizes faith and speculation in favor of observation,
but it would be reckless to state that its observations are
necessarily "logical." Much modern science, anyway, has
dedicated itself to the refutation of conclusions based on

a "logical" interpretation of "known" facts. It may follow logically that if the world can go on without species A or ecosystem B, then that species or system is unnecessary, but that is not a *scientific* perspective. It is merely the end point of a game which, once one knows certain basic rules, is as predictable as tic-tac-toe, without shedding much greater light on the nature of things.

To put it another way, the twentieth century may be remembered in history for the Heresy of the Least, which is to say that we are the first civilization I know of which has tried to make a virtue out of being the least it can be, which has presented behavior shorn of all but the most brutish and self-serving motivation as being "scientific," and therefore both realistic and heartily to be desired. Caution and altruism are all very well as a public mask, but actually sentimental shams fully transparent to the most evolved of our movers and shakers. There is no logical reason why we shouldn't try to get away with as much as we think we can. There is no logical reason why we shouldn't grab for as much as we can hold—for more than we can hold, hiring armies and courts to hold it for us—without regard to who is being dispossessed. Once certain misinterpretations of "natural law" are firmly in place, it is practically a folly not to produce less and charge more, not to lie for advantage, not to take what cannot be defended, not to put your thumb on the scales. It is true that greed works. If that is true, then we good scientists must remember that nature always uses what works, and so should we.

Though I believe there are mighty spirits and powers of light watching over our deeds in the garden of the world, I cannot assert there is any *logical* reason why we should not ream the planet dry of all resources, heaping up treasures for ourselves and letting the future gasp out its life on the shores of poisoned seas. All I can say with certainty is, *That is not who I want to be.*

Ancient man possessed an instinctive grasp of orderly natural succession. Pharaoh dies, but there is always Pharaoh. Assyrians lay down their ravenings; Hittites, Parthians, Gauls come to take their place. A dozen divinities succeed each other at Delphi, but it is still the navel of the world. Solomon says, "There is nothing new under the sun." He does not say, "There is no *one* new." Individuals pass away, the category persists.

Like kings from a Mesopotamian chronicle, the rulers of the former world leave behind a few relics and a pedigree of jaw-cracking names. In the valley where my house stands, camels herded with caribou, saber-toothed cats stalked elephants, raking skin and muscle with their terrible scimitars, staining the snow with blood. Ten tons of sea cow plough the waters of the North Pacific. Hammurabi, or even George Washington, could have seen one had he sailed to the Komandorskie Islands. Steller's sea cow will survive until 1768, when Russian sealers exterminate it twenty years after discovering it. Whatever kelp-gobbler of the Cretaceous it replaced vanished unlamented by either ecologists or sentimentalists.

Backward through the epochs, other predators, other prey: nightmare ratites kicking the guts from proto-ungulates, bipedal sprinting razors, part bird, part dinosaur,

part bad dream, bringing down their victims in a Göt-
terdämmerung of steaming flesh. On the plain surrounding Ur, jackal and lion assume ecological niches once filled
by the lantern-eyed hunters of the Pleistocene. The grace-
ful cheetah of the Persian kings prances out from the skin
of monsters with the heft of bears. Abraham culls his flock
from the unicorns of Eden.

Did the planet notice all this coming and going?
Leopard and Tyrannosaur are, in an ecological context,
the same animal, performing the same labor. Nut-cracker,
bone-gnawer, nectar-sipper are eternal classifications. The
particular inhabitants of those niches are temporary and
contingent. There is always the conqueror, always the
spoiler, always the messiah, though names change and grass
grows over the capitals.

All this is true, I would say to my student. But also, it is
bigger than anything I want to have my hand in. I do not
want to call the figures. I am happy merely to be dancing
the dance.

～

Once I saw a ghost.

Winter light fell on the Texas coast. I was walking
backward, not so you could see, but in time, counting
a generation or so with each step, proceeding out from
motel lobby and beach flotsam, from among pale vaca-
tioners exercising white dogs on sand ground from the
bodies of creatures dead before the empires of man began.
For many yards I hugged the breakwall that keeps the
hurricane storm surge out, sometimes. Meadowlarks gur-
gled on the telephone wires, their feathers sun-colored,

fresh, new mintage in an old, old world. I found the marsh road and took it as far as it was going, into a land filled with tiny voices, with low, metallic pools darkened by long-legged waders. I retreated from the present into a past so remote that I thought I might see something no eye had seen in my time. I believe such things are possible, if only one could desire enough, long enough, wisely enough, if one could find the right resonance of will to shatter the barriers.

The sand yielded under my feet. It was the color of pale butter, of a cougar's pelt. Like the human soul, it took the shape of whatever had last passed over it—wind, the highest ripple of the tide, the little scrabbling prints of crabs. My own tracks, in that world of miniatures, followed me like the spoor of a dinosaur. The air was neither warm nor cool, but so perfectly adjusted to my body as to be impalpable. Something in that impalpable air made me unusually—even morbidly—attentive. I watched the shadow of gulls move over the dune, too huge and silent to be what they were. I believed it would be a day on which I would see something wonderful.

What came of it at last was that I saw two curlews on Galveston Island. They were quite distinct, one smaller and shorter-billed than the other, at a season when size differential was not likely to be the result of age. I knew the larger immediately as *Numenius americanus,* the common long-billed American curlew. But the magic of the day and the strangeness of the winter light led me to hope that the other might be *Numenius borealis,* the Eskimo curlew, a bird rare to the point of the fabulous. By the word of some, extinct.

I had flown to Houston to attend the convention of

the Modern Language Association, an experience, if one thought about it, not unlike a stroll among the highly evolved waders of the Gulf. In the whistling vacancy of the Hyatt Regency Hotel nested the whole biota of a profession: unspecialized, scavenging, starling-like creatures darting into whatever controversy became available, propounding Bentham one moment and Dante the next, ears cocked for sustenance, advancement, or, sometimes, knowledge; hyper-specialized library-fowl, sipping nectar from a single flower only, evolved to precise and brilliant focus, able to say all that's sayable concerning Dryden's use of the tercet, liable to extinction at the burning of a single book; ambitious cuckoos, raucous jays letting the unformed children of their brains be fed to maturity by others, thieving merrily and holding their prizes up for inspection at the next California cash bar; the high-flying hunters, swift to the mark, the hawks and storm-riding Canadas, the arctic-circling albatrosses approaching at great height and great speed, taking in whole quarters of the globe.

After a few days of that particular exhilaration, I felt the need for contrast. I skipped the penultimate session of the convention and took a bus to Galveston for my first look at the Gulf of Mexico. I don't remember anything between Houston and Galveston but brown scrub of identical shape and dimension, though I'll grant that December might not be the land's best season.

I longed to see an armadillo, even a dead one smashed on the road, and kept my nose glued to the bus window. The bus made stops at Texas City. What I knew of that town was that it had once blown up. Egrets stabbed and stalked there in the shadow of the refineries. I suspect the refinery PR office photographs them and calls it an example of the compatibility of nature and industry. I found it a momentary grace.

Galveston I liked for its mixture of fine Victorian architecture and personable, tumble-down informality. I bought a sandwich and was called "hon" three times by people who had never laid eyes on me before. I bought a map. On part of the map lay the streets and blocks and points of interest of Galveston. Beyond that grid lay a great blank dotted with the blue of tide pools. It was that blank I wanted.

A concrete seawall defends the city from the Gulf, and the frontier-creating windward of the wall brims with twittering, creeping life that the punctilious would, I suppose, call vermin. The beach had become a highway for off-road vehicles and motorbikes, and for safety's sake one walked close to the water, sidling into the very waves when some horse-powered hot dog gunned too close. On the public beach, sanderlings pattered in and out of the surf on their clown feet, at once hilarious and, against the immensity of the gray sea, brave and solemn. One grass-green hermit crab had chosen a shell of deep sandy crimson, to an effect of bold elegance.

What from the distance looked like boulders turned out to be tractor tires buried in the sand, gleaming rubbery black in the waves. Sacks of bright plastic electrical components washed up beside sea-monstery lengths of rubber hose, boots, unruffled copies of *Sports Illustrated.* A huge clear bag full of tiny seashells settled on the tiny seashells of the beach. The effect of all the trash was curiously beautiful, the flotsam of Atlantis, cleansed and mysterious.

I turned inland toward the U.S. Fish and Wildlife

laboratory lagoon, startling a blue heron, that deigned to flap a few yards before landing and going on with the hunt. I was not important here. I could be outrun or outswum or outflown by anything I encountered.

The theory that birds are dinosaurs shrunk, feathered, and shot into the sky is never more believable than in clear view of a heron, with its reptilian eye, its un-avian immensity and croak, its air of the primeval. I watched it long and close, a disturbing experience, actually, one that made me a little afraid. I wouldn't want a closer look even had the bird granted it. My apprehension was not physical, but sprung from the *otherness* of the creature stilting about in the lagoon twelve feet away. Only by accident did we inhabit the same world. I was watching time. The dinosaurs I loved so as a child had not passed away, any more than my childhood had. We had all transfigured. They pulled a vanishing act so subtle and thorough that it took us millennia to catch on to it. They transfigured, leapt into the air. The Aztecs with their feathered serpent had looked the heron in the eye. I had become a writer, able to go to absurd places and say tenuous things and make it pass for a living.

My concentration on the heron was so great that I didn't notice the Virginia rail hunting at my sneaker tips. I laughed aloud with the joy of seeing her merry in the sedges, poking and probing, wading boldly toward the center of the lagoon, but never so far that the westering winter sun left her in too high a relief against the water. I don't think I could have spooked her with anything less than a buck-and-wing. Never quailing from the specter of anthropomorphism, I contend that the rail's expression was much homelier and more readable than the heron's, and what it expressed was satisfaction. For some of us, one salt pond is sufficient world.

Across the dirt road lay a much larger pond, where visibility was reduced, paradoxically, by a superabundance of light. Glare from the surface flashed golden and blinding. Even in the flash I could see that the pond's surface was strewn with the shadows of waders. I edged down to the shore. Amid the shining, I seized on the unmistakable silhouette of a curlew. To the curlew's left and nearer to me paused another shadow, like the curlew's, but smaller, just over half its size, not an avocet, not a whimbrel, not a— what else was there? My heart leapt at the thought that I might be seeing the Eskimo curlew.

I took a chance that these birds too might be infected with the tameness of the rail and the heron. I crept along to get a vantage point without the sun in my eyes. The birds did not move. I knew the same light which blinded me must be lighting me up like a moving Christmas tree, and that any attempt at stealth must be, in the birds' eyes, ludicrous. I reached the desired angle, whipped out my camera, swiveled the lens onto the bird. It was too far away. Though I could see the birds well enough, the curlews shrunk to sticks in the viewfinder. Had to get closer. Had to wade into the pond if necessary.

That was a mistake. The instant sneaker touched water, the birds flew, calling, the little curve-bill shearing off from the path of the big one, and I too occupied with fishing myself from the drink to note where they had gone.

On top of everything else, I had read the schedules wrong, and arrived at the station as my bus belched toward the Houston Road. I had to run to catch it, then sit sweaty and breathless, unable to share with any of those faces the tale of my travels back through time.

"I saw a bird," I might say.

They would smile, half turn to the window, wanting to be left to their own thoughts.

"An *Eskimo curlew!*"

They'd turn fully now, pretending to watch the toss of refinery lights on the egret-y water.

I returned home on New Year's Eve, where, researching in my bird books, I discovered that the last reliable sighting of the Eskimo curlew had been on Galveston Island. I called the local Audubon hierarchy, whose opinion was that it was the wrong time of year for a sighting in Texas, that if the poor creature existed at all, it would be padding the shores of Patagonia.

This opinion did not sway me. I had seen what I had seen.

Unless—unless it was something more amazing still. Unless I had seen a ghost.

We've all had the experience of talking to a friend in a bookstore or on a street corner, and late in the night the phone call comes announcing that he is dead. Tidings of the curlew moved me in the same way. Had I seen the last one on earth, who chose to pass his days in peace on that prow of muck rather than risking Patagonia a final, futile time? Had I seen the shade of a creature already passing from the realm of human credulity?

Extinct has an oddly clinical ring to it. A mishap, it sounds, a slip of the evolutionary pen. The word does not do justice to a calamity exceeding the human imagination, which had experienced, which faces in any foreseeable future, no such thing. I thought I would be content to know the curlew to be, beyond a doubt, extinct, content to know I had seen the ghost of a bird where it had flourished in life, passing as hesitantly and lingeringly from its ancient home as human ghosts are said sometimes to pass from theirs.

I went to Houston to get a job in academia. I did not get one, then. Usually I resent having to think of good things as compensation for better things denied, but in the case of the curlew, it was enough.

The coda to the story is that in 1982, two years after my "sighting," there was a documented sighting of the Eskimo curlew. Perhaps there have been more. Perhaps one of them was of my individual. Perhaps we are all deceived, and the bird, like the dinosaurs, has pulled a vanishing act so complete and so subtle we cannot yet process the reality of it.

Ground sloths became extinct so recently that in caves in Terra del Fuego their pelts have been mummified recognizably by the freeze-drying atmosphere, hair and fatty tissue intact.

Members of the Russian nobility once dined on Mammoth meat preserved by ice in the high Arctic. People now alive heard in childhood possibly genuine eyewitness reports of the New Zealand moa.

That someone now living will—barring some millennial alteration of attitude—be the last mortal to see a wild rhinoceros or a free-living orangutan is almost a certainty. Something belonging to us and our descendants has been stolen away, and it is almost impossible to determine to whom to complain, what redress to suggest, other than "turn it all around. Abandon what you have begun." Not very likely.

I have, in general, wanted pretty ordinary things. But among the less ordinary desires which have obsessed my heart is that I have yearned with a full, Faustian heart to lay eyes on the creatures of vanished worlds. I covet time machines wildly and irrationally. I want Dr. Who's Tardis to take me backward in history. Any spot will do, for it's not human history I mean, not at first anyway. Napoleon and Saint Paul interest me only marginally—and then mostly to give the latter a good talking-to. But I ache from my marrow to see diplodocus shoulder through the tree-ferns. I want to stand on Pangaea's shore and watch the swan-necks fishing, the great fins at their harvest in the deep. This is not curiosity. This is love unrequited, unfulfilled, an obsession as gaudy as a Tudor tragedy.

A selection of alternate Edens inhabit the brain. Some of them involve realistic expectations and plausible outcomes. Some of them do not. Say you are Adam, and this is the first Garden of the World. Cycads sway in the breeze off the Tethys Sea. A clutch of dragon's eggs gleam like agates on the riverbank. You hear God walking in the cool of the morning. He brings the beasts to you. He brings

the beasts to you so you can give them names. You say,
"panther." You say, "bird of paradise." The panther you
have just half-created scampers onto the golden plain.
The bird of paradise flutters between the chomping, calm
faces of giraffe and indricotherium. The smilodons roar
from the cliffs. The blunt-winged roc-eating eagles blot
the sun. Ramapithicus croons to her daughter in the ar-
caria shade. God giveth all their meed in due season.

Something in this world cuts off the revery. Where are
they gone? You start to grieve, but then you remember
that nothing dies without death's having first become
beautiful to its imagination.

I am not a joiner. My politics are, to put it generously,
subtle. But I manage to do something now and then to
earn the name of environmentalist. Why that, when the
world's suffering offers so many possibilities for concern?
Because I am lonely. Because to imagine my children and
theirs after them calling into a denuded world to the gray
whale and the condor and the rhino, irretrievably depart-
ing even as I write, is a blow deeper than I wish to weather
now. Or ever.

Winter

IMMENSE AND MAJESTIC, the passage of the sun and
the cold comets, the wheeling of the galaxies, the slow
drip and drift of the elements carving canyons, sea-
bottoms, flattening prairies, blowing lakes into steppes
and tundras, chiseling faces in stone, wiping the faces away
and after them the stone they were made of, raising new
stone up, pulling back the swathing of the seas, beginning
the process over again. If I look in one direction, I see that
most everything is slower than I. This is a blessing. I am a
wind at play on the infinitesimal becoming of worlds. I can
help them, hinder them, leave a mark, make a difference.
My imprint can be on the time to come as surely as the
fossil bivalves live out their immortality on the stones of
Clark Reservation. I can extinguish a species, or, leaving
a corner of the garden unmown, lowering the rifle at the
last moment, preserve one into the future.

The woodland ants I disturbed by knocking off a bit of
bark scurry at incredible speed, like a film on fast forward.
They clasp their white grubs in their mandibles, lunging
for the dark, hoping to preserve a generation. My two cats
have grown middle-aged, contented, fat, while I—I like to

believe—have changed not that much at all since bringing them home as kittens. The catbird in the ailanthus tree raises her babies in a frenzy of hunting and gathering in the shadows of the garden. Cosmic rays blast through my skull as I write. Dispensations of bacteria mature, mutate, die, give way to new quintillions in my own gut. I am as unaware of them as is a galaxy of the worms crawling on a little planet of one of its little suns. If I look in the other direction, most everything is slower than I, a race, an accelerated collapse, an impetuosity, a glimmer in the corner of my eye. I cannot possibly get to know anything fast enough. They are grown and gone by the time I cry, "Wait!" I am a pinnacle of rock in a maelstrom, a boulder in a flowing stream, troubling and redirecting what collides with me without their knowing why, how, or by whom they were shoved aside.

When I was a little boy playing along Roosevelt Ditch in Akron, Ohio, I found a boat hook tangled in a bramble thicket. Winter came and I went down to the creek to play, but it was frozen solid. I went back to the garage, fetched the boat hook, and discovered that, with a little sturdy application, I could use it to break through the ice and reveal the still-flowing water below. Now, the importance of that moment was greater than this description reveals. When the ice broke, a sudden gleam shot up from the water, and a sound that seemed to me almost human, almost like song. Then the broken ice slammed into the intact ice downstream. The current forced the broken ice under the dome, and down the fragments went, banging and thumping their way against the bottom of the ice roof. The noise of ice grinding on ice drowned the sound

I knew I heard when the ice broke, so I had to break another fragment to hear it again. It was clearly human,
clearly a song. One or two notes got out before the swirl
of ice and cold water covered the music up, but those one
or two were enough.

Immediately I plumped down in the middle of an
epic. I was a great sun-giant, a god who had heard the
cries of a civilization buried under ice, and had come to
break their prison with blows of the mighty Boat Hook.
I let in the light. I allowed the singing waters to flow.
Though it was a boy's fantasy, I was not all *that* young,
nor was I unaware of the wall between my dream world
and what anybody would see if they wandered to the banks
of Roosevelt Ditch that winter evening. I was playing with
time. I was making a thaw in the depth of winter. I was
rushing the spring I did not know I longed for until I
caught myself beating on the citadels of ice. The flow of
the creek had stopped, and I would start it again. I was
changing the pace of things. I was not a thing whirled
around by time; I was, for the moment, the timekeeper.

When I stopped for a moment and looked up, I saw
that it was nearly dark. Lights were on in the neighbors'
houses. Had they come outside in the cold for a moment,
they could have heard me smashing away at the creek ice.
They could have heard me changing the flow. The light
from the windows caught on something else along the
creek bank. Something upstream from me gleamed,
blinked, went out, gleamed again. When the shapes came
into the open, I saw they were the shapes of raccoons. The
raccoons had heard me, and had come down to the water,
breaking their winter fast by fishing in the stream I had

temporarily opened. The evening was very cold and getting colder; the stream would be closed again before
morning. They would have to work fast.

I hadn't realized how cold I was until I saw the skinny
raccoons pawing around in the near-dark, in the near-
freezing water, exactly like me.

Homo sapiens is a tropical species. African, most likely.
Our first winters were rainy, followed by dry summers,
then spells of profound aridity which lasted for centuries,
driving us down from the withering trees onto the leopard-
haunted veldt. Some of us, to escape the drought, or simply out of curiosity, walked north, where glaciers lay across
Europe and joined Siberia to the New World. What we
made of that Ur-winter is impossible to know now, but
I know that my blood was not yet in the world, for if it
had been we would have turned tail and headed back to
Africa, drought and leopards be damned. Whoever was
there took it into their heads to move deeper north, to wear
the skins of beasts, to let their color change to the color of
the snow and the pale tundra flowers, stopping only when
the frozen continents came to an end.

Now, the fact is, I am afraid of almost nothing. Not of
snakes, not of dogs, not of the night or the night streets.
Phobias are fascinating to me because I have no particle of
understanding of or sympathy for them. But I am afraid
of cold. Not of winter, which is beautiful, but of the ichor
of winter, which is, simply, the Cold. I do not associate it
with discomfort, nor even with death, so much as with
the Immovable—that whose frozen roof must be beaten
open, that whose stymied flow must be freed at whatever
cost. Then the creatures will come down with their bright

eyes to feed. Then I can go to my warm house and drowse with a book in my hand, knowing that I did my part.

~

Here is a mystery. Hiking in the winter in Ohio, after many frosts, even sometimes after snow, I have found clusters of wild grapes on the forest floor, cool but unfrozen, ripe, edible, small, sweet. I have asked people to explain this, but no one has. Of course I have looked for the nearby grapevine. Grapes do not grow in deep woods. Grapes do not grow in winter. Grapes that size do not remain un-eaten in the famished wilderness.

The one useful comment was when someone said, "Did you eat the grapes?"

"Yes."

"Well, then, you were like Elisha, fed by ravens in the wilderness. Not a puzzle, but a miracle."

It isn't profitable to add, "But Elisha had the Lord's work to do," because the obvious response is, "Then so do you."

But what?

Go and find out. Hike past the end of the road, for while you're on the road you're still in control. Go hungry if you can, to invite the descent of the manna, of the inex-plicable fruits. If you were a saint you would go barefoot. Hold your binoculars before you as a monk his begging bowl, wait for something to be dropped in.

As for the nature of the manna, the raven-bread, the unsus-pected sustenance, it can be anything. Moral philosopher William Paley argues for the existence of God by saying that, should one, crossing the heath, strike one's foot against a stone, one might possibly assume the stone came there by happenstance, by the brute jostling of particles in an insensate universe. However, should one tread upon a watch, one would never suppose it had just happened. Reason would dictate the existence of a watchmaker.

Now, this might make good sense as far as the watch is concerned, but it is a terrible slander against the stone. Remember: the silica fleck has descended from the surface of a star. The stone's green mottles are canyons and basins forested with algae. I don't see why a plain old rock doesn't trumpet the existence of a guiding intelligence as well as a machine; or, to put it the other way, why both of them couldn't be witnesses for the amazing potential that lies in atoms simply staggering blindly about for sufficient periods of time.

Recently there had been a to-do about a stone from Mars, and whether some pattern within it did or did not indicate remnants of Martian life. I want to tell the reporters, *Slow down.* I want to dwell on the fact that there is a stone from Mars sitting in a Terran museum, and we didn't bring it here. The bland explanation is that an asteroid slammed into Mars, scattered bits of it across the solar system, some of those bits making it through our atmosphere and crashing into a glacier somewhere, where it just happened to be picked up by a person who wouldn't let it live out the rest of its life as a doorstop. This is a little like my losing a ring from a boat off Bali and having it show up in the belly of the trout I'm eating in Denver six months later. Clearly not impossible, but still miracle enough to stagger sextillions of infidels.

I have a fossil sitting on the base of my lamp. Two

perfect little trilobites crawl over each other, as they have now for half a billion years, frozen in black stone. It is what I think of when someone asks me what is my most prized possession, though, if I remember right, it came from a shop in Charleston for eight bucks. On one trip to Ireland I picked two stones up from Tralee Bay, and carted them with me for the balance of the journey. They sit at my elbow as I type. Both are brownish-grayish, both vaguely oval, one matte, the other sparkling a little with flecks of crystal fire. One is rounded and pock-marked, like an egg, and like an egg, otherwise absolutely featureless. The other is flatter, and has running through it unequal bands, striated against the grain of the rest of the stone in a substance that is tawny, variegated, glittering with crystalline structures. I have no idea what I'm looking at when I'm looking at these stones, except *architecture*.

I am not carrying the banner for God when I make these observations, but for myself. To discover I really am *random* would go against my every perception. It would induce a perceptual chaos from which I could not recover. Certainly a lot of time went into the making of my trilobites, my Tralee stones. We tend to think of gradualness as the opposite of intention, but we are a hasty species. Time is what the universe has. Why not use it?

In 1802 our friend William Paley succumbs to an ecstasy of hopefulness and naivete, writing in "Natural Theology, or the Evidences of the Existence and Attributes of the Deity, Collected from the Appearances of Nature":

> It is a happy world after all. The air, the earth, the
> water team with delighted existence. In a spring

noon, or a summer evening, on whichever side I
turn my eyes, myriads of happy beings crowd my
view. . . . Swarms of newborn *flies* are trying their
pinions in the air. Their sportive motions, their want
on mazes, their gratuitous activity, their continual
change of place without use or purpose, testify to
their joy, and the exultation which they feel in their
lately discovered faculties. . . . Other species are *running about* with an alacrity in their motions which
carries with it every mark of pleasure.

For eight generations, Paley's sanguineness must have pro-
voked howls of derision from the scientific community.
Would it now? Public television nature specials use parsi-
moniously words like "pleasure" and "enjoy" and "beautiful," but permit in the photographing of their subjects a
hue of rapture falling little short of Paley's. To say that animals are driven wholly by instinct and the automatic re-
sponses of the nerves is not more scientific—is in some
degree less scientific—than Paley's terrestrial jubilee, for it
assumes a mystical wall between human experience and
the experience of other animals. It assumes that our experiences of joy and hope and anxiety magically disappear
one step back on the family tree, that what is love or
courage or high spirits in us has been mutated from something lesser, insensate and purely chemical, in them. It assumes that what is visible is not what is, but rather some
other thing is, which conforms to a dogma not demonstrable but fiercely cherished nevertheless. If this is not a
description of faith, I have never heard one.

The idea that my immortal trilobites were not in some

measure enjoying themselves in their life seems a childish
arrogation of all the good things to ourselves.

≈

It's ten degrees below zero, the sky as brilliant as burnished
metal. A student and I walk the frozen Exeter River, to gain
perspectives impossible over liquid, even from a boat. "Frozen" is inadequate to describe the condition of the water;
the river is a gray stone slab ten inches thick, polished by
wind, too glaringly slick to walk on except where blan-
keted by last night's snow.

Suddenly, in this Plutonian cold, we see movement.

A waterscorpion crawls across the ice, its breath tubes
dragged behind, the painstaking Y of persistent interroga-
tion. I kneel to look closer. My companion crushes the
waterscorpion under his boot. Shocked, I rise to confront
him. His face burns with horror. I see now. I am the mon-
strous one. I'll look at anything.

There are certain infernal species, like the bishop pine,
which can complete their life cycle only in the presence
of fire. Thick husks must be charred away, cones must be
coaxed to open to a chorus of hissing needles. Vast areas of
swampland and savannah require flash fires to clear away
the detritus of old growth and let the new appear. The
Everglades would subside into sterile thickets without the
severe cleansing of flame.

I wonder if there is an opposite sort, boreal natures
needing a howling nor'easter and twenty below to come
to an understanding with the universe. For a time I moved

steadily north, from Maryland to New York to New
Hampshire, whenever I could crossing the Portsmouth
bridge into Kittery, so to get still further north. There was
something up there I wanted. Clarity, I think, a landscape
of contrasting light and dark, a country naked and dangerous, the track of the wolf revealed by patches of snow
on bare stones.

Now I live seven hundred miles south and make the
best of it. On bad days in the middle of winter I trot
down to the road to help shoulder my neighbors' sub-
compacts out of the ditches along Chunns Cove. "Not
used to driving in snow," I suggest in my most clipped
Northern accent. I like to see their pink faces, feel their
desperate shoulders pressed against mine under the
bumper.

I think, "I'm not as cold as you," but this is not strictly
the case. Like a fish in an arctic river, it is possible to survive the cold by matching it from within.

When we were kids, we would wait for the first snowfall
and ask our father to drive us to the metropolitan park.
This was a ritual the winter could not proceed without.

Three wide fields punctuated the park forest. One field
was gigantic. It contained the softball diamond and
sported smelly hole-in-a-board toilets and a beautiful
black wood creosote-fragrant picnic shelter. To stand in
its center was perfect exhibitionism, as anyone in the park
could see you, and, alone in the light, you need have no
thought for them. During the winter you'd sled down

Morningview Hill. If you were very skillful, or had one of those cruel black-runnered sleds as long as your body, that the boys from the junior high got for Christmas, you could coast all the way from Morningview to the black wood shelter, which had removable walls and windows for winter, and within which there would be fires and chocolate.

In summer on the field, you played baseball.

I hated baseball, and crossing that field even now brings back memories of confusion and shame. Whether I hated the game because I was not good at it, or was not good at it because I hated it, the memories are nagging and immortal. Why shouldn't I be able to do what every idiot in the neighborhood can do, apparently without effort? A time-lapse film of the big field through the early sixties would find me for significant passages of the summers just standing there as the game unfolded around me. I was known not to be any good, so the ball was rarely thrown to me, and when it flew there of its own accord, expectations were mercifully low. Given those circumstances, I was often quite happy in the outfield, listening to the birds at the edge of the forest, listening to people shouting down by Alder Pond, watching as the blue stars of summer winked on one by one, the newly awakened bats setting out between them on the evening foray. If someone shouted, "Play deep!" for some heavy hitter, I cheerfully did, creeping to the forest edge, my ankles brushed by the umbrellas of the mayapples. I wanted to take the next step. I wanted to disappear into the woods. I figured they'd never miss me.

The second field lay eastward of the big one, and was

medium-sized, too long and narrow for most games, but good enough for church youth picnics. You set the giant, frosty-sided punch keg on the chestnut stump that had been preserved and creosoted as a *memento mori*. Elders grilled hot dogs under the shade at the edge of the field. If you were playing late, the gleam of coals would lead you home. At the other end stood the largest sassafras trees I have ever seen. Generations of kids ripping off their lower branches urged them up until they were the height and almost the girth of forest trees.

The third field lay northward, almost against Alder Pond, small and round in its circle of oak and chokecherry. It was to the third field that one came when the snow fell. Don't ask why. As the first snow was falling, Father would drive to the park and we would run toward the third field. We were in some anxiety to get there, for my sister and I had to be the first to walk in the new snow. We could be first in our yard or first in the great baseball field, but only the third field counted. While my father waited, my sister and I ran to the center of the sacred precinct, not trampling, but cutting evidence of our presence like two tiny booted lasers, in intricate spirals which must have looked from the crowns of the trees like a bolt of paisley. To stand there in heavy Thanksgiving snowfall—flakes big as dollars striking lashes and cheeks—was to know that the season was unfolding right. After a while you would realize it was cold and dark, and father would drive you home.

In the 1880s, George Vanderbilt caused a trail to be blazed from Biltmore House, near Asheville, to Buck Springs hunting lodge on the slopes of Mount Pisgah, dividing seventeen miles of peerless wilderness, over which he reigned uncontested, for a little while. It was a habit of his family to acquire fiefs and empires, and in this, George outdid them all. You can stand on considerable peaks and see nothing but Vanderbilt land in all directions. The trail came to be called the Shut-In trail, perhaps because some of it takes the shape of a green tunnel enclosed by rhododendron thickets, called hells, not because they are unpleasant, but because they are trackless and if you stray from the path, the legend is, you'll never find your way back. The Shut-In trail inclines from about two thousand feet to nearly five thousand feet, passing through land of spectacular variety: brooding cliffs, verdant near-jungles, ridge backs and bogs and waterfalls, as though constructed by Disney as a condensed panorama of the Blue Ridge. What grandees passed along the path in Vanderbilt days is difficult to say, for the forest has forgotten them.

The Shut-In fell on bad times when the estate became private property, and it was severed in several places by the construction of the Blue Ridge Parkway. Boy Scouts and other volunteers restored it, and plan extensions that will enable one to walk from Mount Mitchell to the dizzy gaps of Shining Rock Wilderness. The Shut-In is a masterpiece of unobtrusive utility. Even where it seems to disappear under loam or into the contours of the mountains, it lies firmly underfoot, palpable, unlosable, though sometimes quite invisible. Occasionally, after a rough winter, or at night, one proceeds by a sense of the path, moving as though one were a divinity, by sheer will that the way be where one is going.

One autumn, discovering that I had walked a fraction of it without knowing what it was, I resolved to walk all of it before the New Year. This can be done in one day if one has thirteen or so hours to spend at a throw, and more stamina than I. I walked it piecemeal, from one of its junctions with the parkway to the next.

It is New Year's Eve, early morning, and I have the last four miles to go. Nothing to it, I say, though my eyes tell me it's the steepest march of all, right up the blue side of Pisgah. I run at first, to make some time and stoke the fires. The western sky doesn't look good. I carry my walking stick on whichever side overlooks the abyss, to prong it into the dirt if I start falling. I found the stick in the middle of the path once, driven into the ground by its former owner, as a gift, or perhaps a warning. It's a good stick. Whoever left it found better, or is not coming back.

The trail is in fact very steep. I keep running a little, but then start sweating, a bad idea for winter. I slow. The spirit drains from my nerves. There's something in the atmosphere, something willful and oppressive, as though Pisgah did not want to be climbed that day. I have gone about half the distance I mean to go when the little voice in my ear becomes strident and unavoidable, and what it is saying is, *Go back!* I trot maybe fifty more paces until I realize that the voice means what it says. I turn, with my back to the blue peak, darkening now under a halo of cloud. Even though it's downhill, I'm not running now. The joy has gone out of it. I sit on a log and eat my

tangerine, toeing the peel under leaves to spare the gray
forest the shock of tropical orange. As I suck the last of the
juice from my fingers, the voice is saying, *Run! Now!* I get
up and run. It feels good; it is the right choice. I'm puffing
up the last hill before Beaverdam Gap, where I've left my
car, when I hear the sound of police loudspeakers, mysterious and eerie so far from their proper context. I slow to a
walk. The loudspeakers make me suspicious. A police loud-
speaker makes criminals of us all. But, I'm curious, and
I deer-step over the crown of the hill, my eyes just high
enough to see without being seen. A Parkway Police
cruiser sits idling beside my little silver Ford.

A quick check of my conscience makes it seem safe to
become visible. The ranger waves and says into his radio,
"I've got the gray Escort. We're coming down."

I rather liked the metonymy of "The Gray Escort." I
may use it as a title one day. I begin to ask why, exactly, we
were coming down, when the ranger points west. Fast as a
man running, a bank of black cloud sweeps toward the
mountain. Under it follows a moving whiteness, a shivering veil: snow. A veritable blizzard. The gray Escort and I
roar down the mountain in the cruiser's wake. We wave to
the officers manning the swinging Parkway gate, who are
there to let us through. We are the last off the mountain
before the storm. It is delicious.

Picture this, how one thing leads to another: Tibet exposed a little more carbon-dioxide-gobbling stone, a volcano covered the sky with ash a little too long—and before

anyone was quite aware, the glaciers once more ground their slow thighs into motion. Most everybody left long ago, but you couldn't quite believe it. You stayed. You chained your tires, checked and rechecked the four-wheel drive, stoked the antifreeze, liking the idea of being last. Then, over the roofs of the town, glittering under starlight like a wall of glass . . .

. . . You wake in the middle of the night. You've heard the sound before, but never so close. The lights flicker, flash back on. But you've been warned. You dress. You wear everything you own. You run out into the knee-deep snow of the front yard. Snow falls so thick that at first you don't notice the glacier, six blocks away, grinding, downhill, southward, at the pace of a man walking. A lone dog barks furiously, backing and snarling as it confronts the Thing moving in the night. You gather your belongings, quickly, realizing that though you'd said you were staying, you had from the first known you would have to leave, and you had planned this exit, subconsciously, mapping routes, packing the car in your head time and time again . . .

. . . That sound is the Methodist steeple crashing, a weird, lone bleat from the organ before the ice swallows them up. *That* sound is its smooth glide onto Main Street, kissing the power lines into oblivion. The lights go out forever . . .

. . . You run into the yard, plowing through the snow, cramming in a few last possessions. The lone dog hangdogs beside you, his bravado chilled. You throw out the Crock-Pot and a hamper of old clothes to make room for him. He curls beside you in the front seat, shivering. You watch while your house bows forward, pushed from behind by the ice. You hit the road, swerving and slipping despite the chains. The dog sleeps, trusting you far more than you trust yourself. You drive. You keep ahead of the ice. Your fingers ache from their death-grip on the wheel. Finally, ahead, a light, at once morning and the last rim of the snow clouds. You ease onto the main highway, give it some gas, startle the dog awake on the seat beside you. You've made it, the two of you; you were the last. The people who stood all night looking northward with worried faces wave as you pass, then turn back northward, as though you were not what they expected. You roll down the window. The air smells of flowers.

〜

My grandmother told me that you can survive exposure to a winter night if you keep dancing. This turns out to be quite true. Whatever you do, don't lie down. The narrow teeth of the starving await what lies down. Move south, move down, but move. Be in a terrible hurry. Warm the lungs. Blaspheme as though your life depended on it. Raise the temperature. In any case, keep dancing.

〜

The first time I saw the aurora borealis was in Ithaca, New York, where I had gone from Syracuse to sing Machaut at a festival of ancient music. Six of us crammed into the director's car, cold and exhausted from our labor in the mills of art. When the car stopped, we unpacked grumpily, like people getting out to inspect a flat.

The director pointed up, asked, "Is that the aurora?"

I combed my experience for what else it could be. I

didn't want to be fooled. This was too important. Blue draperies shivered in the northern sky, stars twinkling behind them. Sometimes the draperies compressed until they were thin streamers, the hair of albinos in deep water. Sometimes they filled the sky, top to bottom, a wall of quaking light.

"Yes," I said, "it is the aurora."

Someone added, "Or nuclear war."

I considered this. It was possible, though Syracuse was all that lay to the north until you come to Montreal, and I doubted that either of those would go first. As I watched the light, I heard a voice, familiar, yet long absent. It was my mother's voice, saying at the back of my brain what she would have said had she been standing there:

"You will remember this night always."

I looked. I drank it in. I made the others wait for me.

～

Day after day, winter persists. Like those bad old times under the ice, spring has arrived by the calendar, but everything remains silent, motionless. New Hampshire's Squamscott River is a plain of ice. I do not have the boat hook anymore, and, besides, it was nowhere big enough. Trees on the riverbank glitter as though glass-encased. The wind bangs their frozen branches into hollow music.

But there is another sound. I hear it twice before I believe my ears and look. It is the rattle of kingfishers. Across the stone river, a pair of belted kingfishers scream and hover, shaking the willow-wrecks into rainbow when they land. They have come back too soon, surely. The river—the whole world—lies frozen. There's nothing to eat. The

Squamscott, though hardly a great river, is not Roosevelt
Ditch. I can't break it. I jump up and down on the gray
ice, but it does not respond in any way, and the sound of
it makes me afraid. I call to the birds to tell them to go
south, but they aren't listening. My imagination watches
them starve. Their blue goes out like snuffed flame.

That night I dream of kingfishers. In the dream, they
hover over a river of crystal, lying motionless, dead and
silent, a door of ice, locked. The birds scream and hover
over the ice. Finally, they climb almost too high for me
to see. From the middle of the air they stoop like falcons,
their jeweled wings held back, dive-bombing the blank
face of the river. When they hit, shards of ice fly up like
diamonds, falling back on the face of the river, rolling,
still moving when the next bird hits, and the next spray
of crystal hits the ice. Up and down, again and again,
inexhaustible.

When I wake from the dream it is still night, or at least
still dark. Something woke me—a sound. I listen for what
the sound was. It is rain, not just a polite spring drizzle,
but a torrent, a cloudburst, rippling down my window as
though it were a creek bed. Black sheets of water dive from
the roof, as the gutters are too slow to carry it. Under the
clap of rain sounds the rifle-shot of the river ices cracking,
heaving like mountains in a time-lapse movie of Creation.
The Squamscott pours over Exeter dam, swirls under its
lean-to of trees, racing to the sea.

Spring.

I know if I got up and ran to the river in the black rain
I would see—at least hear—the kingfishers diving like
thunderclaps, flying up, laden with fish.

Weasels

Some animals are not *just* animals. I have known this for a long time. When I was five, my father built a garage. Driving into the garage at night, your headlights illuminated the back wall and the wood beams where he stored tools. One night the headlights set ablaze the lantern eyes and undulating body of a weasel, which paused for a moment, baring its teeth in a snarl of defiance before disappearing into the complexities of the ceiling. I'd awakened from a sound drive-home sleep in the back seat of the car at just the right second, opened my eyes at the one lucky angle that revealed a weasel in the rafters. Nobody else saw it, or, as it turned out, believed that I had seen it. Weasels were creatures of the wildwood. That one could live in our garage was something mother and father did not want to face. But I saw it and knew it wasn't a rat or a squirrel, which were the more modest alternatives suggested. I never saw the weasel again, but likewise never did I enter the garage without believing that a pair of blood-colored eyes was trained on me, drilling into my skull with messages from the night. That the messages were then, and are still, unclear doesn't matter at all. I wait.

~~

Bob Dolittle introduced me to New York's Morgan State Forest one Thanksgiving. The idea of hiking on Thanksgiving was new to me, though it was a long tradition with him. I lived with tiresome people then, and thought it would be good to get away on a holiday, when the tiresome tend to be at their worst, so I packed my knapsack and off we went. I would be back when it was time to pick the cold bones of the turkey carcass.

We hiked in gaudy hats, singing filthy songs as we went, so hunters would not mistake us for deer. That day it was just the two of us, though on fair, bright days we'd pick up Bob's friend Jaime, the painter, so he could look at the bare colors of the northern Appalachian winter, and Jaime's girlfriend, Annie, a potter, with the imperturbable serenity which seems to come with that craft. The four of us made a din no hunter could mistake. Jaime was a demon for fire-building, and twice in a hiking day we'd huddle around a fire he'd conjure from snow in five minutes, his long hands red and bare to the cold. Annie pulled packets of cocoa and other delicacies out of, apparently, thin air. Bob knew where we were going. I—well, I was a *guest*. I didn't have anything to do, wasn't expected to do anything but amble along. It was wonderful.

After I learned the trails a little I started going there by myself. Sometimes I didn't even get out of the car, but just sat a minute at the turn-off with the engine ticking before returning to my duties in Syracuse. The chickadees said, *Hello,* and, *Goodbye,* with a single whistle. They'd call my name at morning and at evening with their melancholy descending whole steps, *David . . . David.* I suppose anyone with a trochee for a name can claim the same.

So, by the time I needed to, I knew where to go. I went, of course, alone, packing on autopilot, without a sense for what would really be necessary. I included two quarts of Canadian Club whiskey, blankets, snowshoes, a walking stick Bob had found for me along a frozen river—no food, no map, no matches, meaning to go hiking, but not to come back.

It had been a bad year, a sort of pendant hanging at the end of a string of bad years. I was still young enough to believe that it would never get any better, and that I couldn't stand it if it didn't. In some ways, I was right. That it doesn't matter much now is a kind of victory, but also a kind of defeat. One gains endurance, loses vision. One does not automatically assume the ledgers balance.

It was beautiful driving into the afternoon of my last day. I was exhilarated and melancholy at once, like a character in a movie. Everything was a portent, the angle of trees against the slope of the hills, birds seen, birds not seen, the slow shadowing of the sun by snowclouds. I had only the poet's regret of not being able to write it down, of not somehow preserving what would be my only perfect poem.

I locked my car at the turn-off, put the keys into my pocket, hating for a dramatic gesture to turn preposterous at the last moment.

I leave the road, hike up, in. The slope is steep. The best athlete gets winded the first few minutes of hiking in deep snow, and I hit the midpoint of the slope before my breath steadies. After that, it's fine. Chickadees call my name in whole steps from the limbs of hemlocks. It's late afternoon, the sun at my back, not warm, but pouring out a blue-white illusion of warmth over the crisscross of squirrel and titmouse tracks, my own snowshoes galumphing amid them like the slither of a great ice serpent. I fist my hands inside my gloves, draw in my fingers to keep them warm.

The going's easy at the top. I relax, spread my legs and move, like a sailor home from the sea. I run the high ridge, the great spine of the folded range. I remember to use my hips, plowing the snow, like a dolphin through water. I run enough to keep warm, but not enough to sweat, which would chill me again. Deer hate the top of the ridge, where their silhouettes stand stark against the sky. I like it. I know if I flew from here, I would beat out and not touch land until the Urals.

Bob had shown me that if you stop at certain places in winter and whistle, the mountain whistles back. It is not an echo, I think, and it doesn't work with a shout, but only with something high and thin, a bird's call or a human whistle. I hit one of those places first try. I stop, whistle. The trees whistle back. I don't know how—a reverbera-tion in the hanging ice? All that sounding board of ripe wood for acres around? The answer is in a different key from my whistle, high and glassy. I whistle as I snowshoe, the Answerer trailing me like the Ancient Mariner's ice spirit guiding his ship from the Pole.

The clouds are very high and break westward, so it begins to snow without the sun's dimming before it sets. I set the memory of the red-gold beauty of the snow into my brain. I think, *Soon I will have no memory,* and hold onto this one, as appropriate, maybe, for the last.

I aim for a hollow under a snag of lumber, one clear of deep snow even now. I have seen it before, perhaps, but I think I am drawn to it by instinct. Before my ancestors sailed to Ireland they must have lived among the snowfields for thirty thousand years. Even I must remember a little of that. There it is. A few minutes' scratching about makes it ready. I lie down. Snow is flying outside now. I unlace my snowshoes, put them outside for a marker. I pull the blankets from my pack, wrap my feet, settle back.

I arrange the two quarts of Canadian Club on the ground beside me, so the second will be in reach when I am blind drunk from the first. For some reason I have brought a mirror, or it still rode in the pack from another occasion, which I tie to a stick directly overhead, so I'll be able to watch my own exit in the settling dark.

The funny thing is that I have never drunk whiskey before, not without its being laced with mixers, and it turns out I hate the taste of it. I sip it gingerly, making faces for the benefit of the mirror above me in the snowcave. But I keep at it, sip after sip. Chemical warmth begins to tickle my nose. The need to shift around to get comfortable diminishes. I need to piss, but it's too cold and I can't move, so I let go where I lie. I want to sleep. I mean to sleep. I keep drinking. I feel myself going blank, cheered because I think I have drained one of the bottles dry, and am not

even sick. Then I sleep. I hear myself trying to say something . . . *B* . . . *B* . . . *B* . . . even I don't know what it is.

Sometime later—maybe a day, maybe half a day—a
sensation comes, a dim uneasiness, like a too-hot bath
stayed in too long. I am waking up. It's not a disappointment—rather the opposite—until I remember why I
am there. It's neither dark nor bright in the snowcave.
Enough light filters through the snowy roof to show the
full bottle of whiskey kicked on its side at my boot tip, the
empty one—I really did empty it, at least, except for the
thin crescent-moon of amber-gold at the very bottom—
propped on a hillock of snow at my elbow. The beauty of
that crescent of amber-gold fills me with melancholy. I am
still thinking I drank enough, lay in the cold long enough,
to die, and now I don't especially want to, and that one
color gleaming in the dark seems a condensation of all the
vanishing beauty of the world. I should cry, but I am too
drunk. Realizing I'm passing out again is a relief. I go out
thinking, *This time for sure!*

I enter a period of alternate waking and sleeping.
Awake, I know I should reach for the second bottle and
drain it, that I should throw the blankets off me, but I am
unable to move. I wonder why I haven't frozen in the night,
why I am not dead—or perhaps I have and I am, and if so,
that too is a terrible disappointment.

Dreams unfold in the periods of stupor. I concentrate
on them to see if they are different from the dreams I had
when I was alive. In one there is a beautiful forest, like the
one around me, but green and sweet with spring. I have
food, crackers that enlarge when taken from the box into
great white cakes the size of baseballs. When I hold them

up, animals crawl from the shadows, golden animals with the habits and dispositions of squirrels, but bird-like in the vividness of their color. Gleaming like little suns, they nibble the cakes from my hand. This goes on a long time. When I give them the last of my magic crackers, I realize my own hunger, and that there is nothing left to eat. It is not mere hunger, but a mule kick to the gut, an agony. In the dream I bend over and moan.

In real time, this was me vomiting against the far wall of the snowcave.

Finally, in the dream, the hunger is so unbearable that I crush the crackerbox to baseball size and hold it aloft as though it were yet one more cracker. One of the golden animals scampers from the trees. It stretches up from the forest floor, reaches with gentle ape hands for the box. It doesn't seem to recognize the ruse, for it nibbles the crushed box contentedly while I pet it, gently, then boldly, careful to caress every part of its body. I clamp my fingers around its neck. It keeps on nibbling. I squeeze. Still it is oblivious, and its obliviousness infuriates me. I swing its body against tree trunks, whirling left and right until its head explodes. Arcs of blood fly through the air and darken the golden fur. Fury and hunger burn my innards. I bite through the fur, spit, bite again, close my teeth on bleeding flesh.

I wake. It is pitch dark. I smell the vomit. I want to sleep again, and begin sinking toward unconsciousness, but a cold fear grows at the back of my skull, until the fear becomes conviction: I am not alone in the snowcave.

How long I lay paralyzed with whiskey and sickness and panic I am not sure. Eventually a halo of illumination seeps in from the outside, rendering the outline of my pack. With infinite stealth I reach in, clutch the cold cylinder of my flashlight, aim at the far corner of the den, snap it on. Between my knees, touching the flesh under denim cuffs when I move, is a weasel. Starved for any morsel in the middle of winter, it is eating my vomit.

I snap the light off and lie back. *Let him feed,* I think. I am so grateful to be of *some* use to *something.* I feel such tenderness toward the little, hungry animal, and then I am once again asleep.

When I wake the final time, gray light fills the snow-cave. The sound from outside underlines the fullness of my folly. It is rain, a January thaw. I stare at the weasel tracks among the vomit stains on the floor. For a moment I feel like laughing.

Oddly, there is no hangover. Perhaps I ejected it in time. I feel dizzy more from hunger than from alcoholic insult. I crawl from my snow den, stand and work fingers, toes, nose, to see if they have been frostbitten or nibbled by the weasel. I tie on the snowshoes—they'll be hell on the alternate slush and glare ice that the rain is turning the mountain into—repack my pack, frugally packing both full and empty whiskey bottles, the second of which I drank over the next six months in infinitely small increments poured into whipped cream and coffee, still hating the taste, still thinking I had to savor every humiliating drop. I shuffle down the mountain which I never meant to leave, cold and hungry in a wilderness of rotting snow. Wild with thirst, I scoop the slush into my mouth. It tastes of moss and metal.

My little car sits at the turn-off, waiting. I pick notes

from under the wipers, notes from forest rangers concerned for the owner of the rusty Toyota. The texts have
disintegrated in the rain. I drive from the forest, worrying
about fuel—but reluctant to stop anywhere, because I smell
so bad—worrying about the rent and missed classes, about
what day it is really, small matters again effervescing in my
consciousness. I unlock my door at sunset on the fourth
day since I'd gone to the mountain. I throw my clothes in
a corner, shower, sleep real sleep.

In the morning I remember that I'm hungry. I've left
the kitchen window open, and the floor is covered by a
delicate veil of snow, so even and thin that I think the tiles
have faded until I touch them with my bare feet.

The Doe

IF THEY SAID TO YOU, "Tell us the last time you remember believing everything would turn out right,"
you would think back to the summer of the mockingbirds, when bounty in the north or disturbance in the
south sent them by the scores into Ohio farmlands, where,
once, people thought themselves lucky if one sang in
a county. You would think of the locust trees, and the
mockingbirds singing in them, the perfume and the
whiteness and the music together. It made you change
your notions about what is too little and what is enough.

You would remember evenings best. The farm women
came out with pitchers of lemonade, and kerchiefs to wipe
their foreheads, and sat on the front porch swings, listening. Supper dishes would keep. The mockingbirds chased
the cats all day, then perched in the lilac until the stars came
out. Farm women climbed to their rooms early, unwound
their hair from scarves and pins, pewter and silver and
crystally Bakelite, their men watching them.

That was the summer it didn't rain until the hay was
in, didn't frost until the tomatoes were played out and the
zinnias arranged safe and scarlet on the sideboard. The

black onyx Seth Thomas clock, whose glass face always clouded in wet weather, was fooled into staying clear right to Thanksgiving.

That was the fire-scare summer, when the black loam of Hartville burned like paper, and the wind was toward us, so we stood by our fathers with hoes in hand to ditch our land safe at the first sign of burning. All that came, finally, was a golden cloud at sunset.

That was the summer my old friend Jack and I hiked down to the creek nearly every day. The creek issued from a storm sewer under Sullivan Street, where the houses ended, and vanished into a storm sewer under the B&O tracks, where the land was wild and the high grass exploded with the cawing of cock pheasant. Between the Sullivan culvert and the railroad dicks, whom we seldom saw but who were rumored to bludgeon first and ask questions later, the creek divided a ragged woods glistening with broken glass, haunted by derelicts who slept it off there, away from the cops and the neighborhood dogs. We caught crayfish and hung them on our shirts to terrify the girls. The crayfish bent their tails over their rumps of eggs and could live forever out of water, waving their claws from the dust balls under our beds.

That was the summer when cloudbursts washed shrews from their burrows in the bank. Jack and I picked tiny drowned bodies from the water, examining them carefully, believing them to be preliminary models, sketches in flesh rather than full animals. Their teeth were bared like stiff white thread. Someone told us shrews were poisonous. We scoffed at the notion, though it turned out to be quite true.

That was the summer when mother took sick. The old folks always said "took sick," as though it were something chosen, like bric-a-brac from a shelf. Once before, when I was very young, she had taken sick and stayed that way so long that I didn't remember her, and the word *mother* took on an abstract resonance, like *Brazil* or *alabaster,* things heard of but hopelessly remote.

They thought it would be easier if she left for the hospital when I was at school. When I got home, Mother would be gone, and I was expected to accept that as though a bowl had been dropped and broken and a child might never notice it at all. It was a mistake, but so, I knew, would be my protest, or even my inquiry. I embarked, therefore, on a program of silent watchfulness that is a hallmark of my nature to this day. Never protest. Never confess what you're watching for, but watch, watch, watch. Mrs. Dodd, from church, was there to take me home with her. Mrs. Dodd asked if I would like milk and cookies. Never in my life had I had milk and cookies after school, the way kids did on TV, and I burst into tears. I thought mother was dead. I thought the milk and cookies were to make up for my being an orphan. Ashamed to have made Mrs. Dodd so miserable, whatever my own status, I calmed down and ate her cookies.

I was too young to visit mother in her hospital room, but sometimes father brought me to the street below, and she would wave from her window. What gave me so low an opinion of the candor of adults I don't know, but I believed firmly that she was gone, and that father had gotten a nurse to put on mother's pale robe and stand at the window and wave to me.

Dreams came to me, of a figure in white satin, who spoke with Mother's voice but moved like movie stars, in the haze and violins that surrounded them in sentimental films when they kissed their children goodnight. When she came home I cried and pulled away, because I did not know her.

People say you can get over anything. I doubt she got over that.

Just before school started in the fall—I had no use for a calendar, but you could tell by the changed light at evening, slanted and golden—I came in from playing, and found Mother with her chair set solidly against the kitchen wall. I stared at her steadily, thinking there was something in the scene I wanted to keep forever. She motioned me to her. She stood me between her knees so she could trim my hair for school. The shears went snip snip right against my ears. I felt her gathering my red hair in her hands so it wouldn't mess the floor. When she finished, she said my name in a funny way. It made me afraid, so I wouldn't look at her. I heard her, though. She was crying.

Mother recovered that time and lived productively for fifteen more years, though ever with an aura of fragility, as though she were the northernmost of some rare, tropical bird, and each shift of wind, each creeping chill filled the heart with dread. When she sickened again, she was the only one not afraid.

She died at winter's end. I lived in Ithaca, New York, then, working as a janitor and living in a trailer. I walked to the bus station with sleet waving over the tops of my shoes. Laughing, arm-punching young men smoked in the back of the bus. The seat beside me was occupied by a

stout babushka-ed immigrant woman who ate her single
thick sandwich over the course of two hundred miles by
poking into the bag with two gnarled fingers, and remov-
ing, like an avocet probing under a rock, the smallest possible fragment. Perhaps she thought if she pulled the whole
sandwich out and took a bite, someone might ask her to
share. Perhaps she thought she would be murdered or put
into a camp because of envy for her sandwich. I hated her.
I hated her for the tragedies and sorrows she went through
that made her think she could eat her sandwich that way.
I hated her because she was afraid and confused and antique and tried to cram too many ripping sacks under her—
our—seat, so my knees had to stick out into the aisle. I
hated her because I couldn't be alone for one moment with
my sorrow, but had to hear the *rattle, rattle, rattle* of two
liver-spotted stubs of fingers striving to sink undetected
into a greasy bag.

I wanted to scream, "My mother is dead and I am
going home for the funeral." I thought the drama would
beautify us all.

I spent much of the spring that followed hiking on
weekends and on days I could spare, or at least *did* spare,
from writing my dissertation. I preferred to go alone. Some
details of that melancholy time stand in memory like figures cut in diamond. Others are lost forever. Days went
by from which I remembered nothing. I would come to
with my feet propped up on the steam register, as though
I had come into being, without a past and without a
memory, at that very moment. On a day when the clouds
hung motionless in the north, like a roof half-finished, I
climbed in Pratt's Falls Gorge.

It was cold at the bottom of the gorge, still deep winter there, away from the sun, but pleasant after the sweaty scramble down. I'd taken a feeder-creek bed most of the way, wading in high green boots, breaking the ice sometimes, sometimes cautiously borne upon it, down the little water to the big one, the river that shoots over Pratt's Falls. In a pool of the feeder-creek I stepped on the body of a frog, awakened too soon, maybe, or dug from his bed by thawing water.

At the bottom I leaned on snow that made an abrupt shelf on the rocky shingle of the stream. It came into my head to sleep there, so I might say I had slept in snow, but it was still too cold. I pulled out my brown-backed notebook and began to draw the tiny trees of lichen I saw on a well-sunned log, like miniature cacti, or foliage in a book of dinosaurs. I drew liverworts gemming the same log like cabbages in a field. Beneath them, tiny black and red spiders scurried about, not deigning to notice me even when I bent in close. I was a mountain, a god, alternately blocking and bestowing their sun.

I'd seen Cooper's hawks over the near gray hill, and I tried to draw them too, but I hadn't seen them close enough, and realized I was drawing my memory of their picture from the Golden Press bird guide. Had I seen them only once, I might have mistaken them for herons, flapping un-hawk-like on their silver wings.

I discovered I could draw with my gloves on. They were my spring gloves, and not too bulky, and my drawing didn't require great delicacy of line, being mostly to remember by. I'd finished the details of the log, and began looking for something else. Wrens fussed by the water, tails up, shrieking sometimes only against me, sometimes in fury at all the creatures of the world. I tried to concentrate on them, but my eyes were drawn repeatedly from bird and stick into the stream itself, from the particular and sketchable into the numinous water. I shifted from looking to seeing without noticing the transition. Drowsy, I stared, then realized I had been staring for a long time.

I brought myself suddenly to, and when I did, the object I had been staring at shook into focus. It was a dead doe, caught in a tangle of wood in the stream. Perhaps she had fallen from the falls, or had been swept from the forest in a flash flood. Shot, maybe, on the bank, and got tangled up there in her last throes. She was so thoroughly involved in the debris that I couldn't tell where her legs were. Everything under the water was stripped clean of hair, until the skin shone smooth and ghostly, like an unborn doe in her mother's belly. Her back was lifted above the current by the snag, and was still furry. Her body was grotesquely contorted, elongated in the direction of the current. Still, the doe was not a horrible sight, bobbing there, but simply startling. Then sad. Then, inexplicably, beautiful. I got up to kick the snag a few times, but it did not release her. Spring rains were around the corner, I decided. They would wash her down.

I walked on and found a path leading up. I didn't turn around, didn't allow myself to think overmuch of the deer at all. But that night when I dreamed, it was of her. In the dream, I kicked the snag away, and she broke free, swimming to shore, bounding into the forest. It was so bare I could see her running for a long time.

That was the summer I could lie on my belly under the

osier bush, reading, hour after hour, drowsy in the sun
that seemed never to move, and the mockingbird came
to sing over my shoulder, rocking the branch when he
landed, and I thought that meant I would be lucky.

A Firmament of Waters

SIX FEET LONG, a torpedo of lean, silver malice, the
shark emerged at the end of a fisherman's pole from
the surf where I had just been swimming at Avalon, New
Jersey. I reached over to touch it, and when I did, I pulled
my hand away raw from contact with the emery-board
skin. Lodged between two of the monster's teeth was a
band of untarnished brass, a boat fitting, perhaps, bent
unrecognizably by the power of those jaws. The fisherman
worked the brass out for salvage. As he did, the shark's
head moved slightly, as though to get a better view of the
procedure.

I said, "It's still alive."

The man with his hand in the creature's mouth said,
"Sure, will be for an hour or two, unless—" He took a
long knife from his coat pocket and offered me the honor
of finally dispatching his catch.

I stood back afterward and wondered who had
thought of this thing, all this hideousness and splendor
compact under one skin. He had once cousins sixty feet
long, whose gape could admit an automobile. Very old
great white sharks, which avoid the shore and contact

with humans, keeping to the un-navigated emptiness of the deep sea, are believed by some to reach unknown dimensions, to achieve an unknown span of years, to devour unknown prey.

Ad majorem Dei gloriam?

～

I first saw whales in the Atlantic off Portsmouth, New Hampshire, despite steady September rain and premonitions of seasickness. Several dozen people, lavaliered with cameras and binoculars, assembled on the wharf awaiting passage aboard the *Viking Queen,* each of us having paid thirty bucks to enter the empire of the Leviathan. Scowling dark men stood spread-legged behind hot-dog cookers, braced and defiant. We would have hot dogs whate'er betide. The ship slid down the Piscataqua toward the sea, and even as it lurched into motion, the clouds parted, and the sun fell across the water like a scatter of new coins.

The Piscataqua River between Maine and New Hampshire is torn by one of the swiftest tides in America, and our passage from river to sea involved palpable violence. The outgoing water churned back on itself like a collapsing wall, its slurry presided over by a wheel of gannets.

This being an Audubon excursion, we were well supplied—oversupplied, if the truth be known—with birders. Black smudges on the waves were identified with dizzying dispatch as scoters, eiders, great and double-crested cormorants, two swift merlins disdaining to take harbor in our rigging, loons (both common and—though there was dissension from the verdict—arctic), northern phalarope, a flock of black-bellied plovers, gulls so plentiful we sighed with ennui when they flapped in sight of our scopes. Birding is one of those pursuits requiring an imperial presence. Two good birders can haggle all day over a shape small and dark and too far away, but in the presence of a master, everyone goes to school. Fate blessed the *Viking Queen* with two such masters, which in a way was the same as having none at all, for when the two made differing identifications, though there would be factions supporting one or the other, there could be no court of final appeal. One of the master birders was lean and cheekboned in a grave black costume, black watch cap pulled low over glittering eyes, a dramatic presence stationed at the topmost projection of the ship, scanning the horizon, neck festooned with lenses. The other was an aging roaring boy, tubby, vivacious, the gravedigger to his colleague's Hamlet, braying out the names of birds with hopeful alacrity, willing to be corrected by the other's cautious, "Now, Walt," the crowd's favorite, for his scarlet coat and war stories of birding expeditions past. The severe one looked with intensity through his lenses, not opening his mouth until the identification was sure; the jolly one barked out the names with suave assurance of what *should* be there, whether he had quite seen it or not. Journeymen occasionally made identification coups, and we all rushed headlong, binoculars clamped to faces, toward whatever side of the boat the action favored.

The sea roughened. The *Viking Queen* rolled sideways into troughs whose crests rose sixteen, twenty feet above our decks—green mountains, translucent, like jade amber hardened around the bodies of fish. I did make a first sighting of my own, rather far down the scale of things, as it was not a bird, but wonderful nevertheless to me: seven ugly feet, easy, of shark, dark green above, pale below, with a blunt, coarse visage, confirming one's supposition of piscine stupidity by swimming smack into the side of the boat. I tallied up the probable number of passengers who would rather see a shark than a gannet, and promoted myself to journeyman wave-watcher.

Despite the beauty of the birds, we'd come for whales, and after a few false starts, we saw them.

Archaeocetes—ancient whales—appeared in the Eocene, fully whales, fully adapted to oceanic life. There are no fossils which can be truly denominated "transitional"; today a bear (or whatever), tomorrow a whale. I dwell on this fact because of my love for the swift and catastrophic. I want the mind of Evolution to be that of a poet, proceeding by furious intuition as much as diligence and patience.

From archaeocetes sprang odontocetes, the toothed whales, including porpoises, dolphins, killer whales, sperm whales, and their like. Slightly later appeared the mysticetes, the baleen whales, a spectacularly successful group that produced the largest animals ever known to exist. Baleen feels like fingernails, but is actually analogous to the ridges on the roof of the human mouth.

The sperm whale, the greatest of planetary carnivores, can hold its breath for an hour, diving to depths of a mile or more in search of squid and other denizens of the benthos, a realm of deep-water blackness and cold less familiar to us than the dark side of the moon. This whale possesses the largest brain on earth. Even its species name, macrocephalus, means "big head." Dinosaurs serve as proof that very large and very complicated bodies can be propelled by, practically speaking, no brain at all, so what the sperm whale has can be thought of as a prodigal super-fluity. What does the whale do with all the gray matter? It echolocates, but so do bats with brains the size of beech-nuts. Some scientists think they actually stun or kill prey with high frequency sonic blasts. That would take another cubic inch or so of brain. What of the rest? What does the sperm whale think about down there in the deep, for only a sentimental behaviorest would deny that the creature does and must think about *something* with all that super-abundance of synapses.

Some scientists believe that the human brain enlarged as a response to our upright posture. Becoming bipedal left our hands free, and our brain, sensing the possibili-ties, began its imperial progress from merely bigger than anybody else's, to needlessly, monstrously huge. Once the habit was acquired, the brain, like a laden cart rolling downhill, kept on in the same direction, getting smarter and smarter, adding jai alai and lace making to the reper-toire of things it could do with its hands—even, with an eye to its own welfare, brain surgery. Perhaps in the same manner, the whale's brain bulked up in order to handle the complicated business of echolocation. Like ours, once it started down the path of giganticism, it saw no particu-lar reason to stop. Our brain can be only so big as to be supported by our necks, while water can support a body of theoretically almost limitless size, which can, theoreti-cally, encase a brain of almost limitless power and subtlety.

So, two big brains divide the planet, one ruling the

land and one ruling the water. One leaves behind it filth and artifacts, the other only a silver wake under the face of the moon. We are who we are because we picked things up from the ground and changed them, fashioned and adapted them to our needs and desires, *Homo habilis,* Handy Man. The other terrestrial brain is, therefore, almost impossible for us to understand, for it is Mind without Manipulation.

Finally we did see whales off the New England coast, first among them the great mahogany finbacks, which reach lengths of seventy feet, weigh eighty tons, and live up to a hundred years. The finbacks are an oddity in the animal world in being asymmetrically colored, the right side of their jaws and baleen being white, and the left side dark. Some believe that this is so the finback can swim in tighter and tighter circles, concentrating its tiny prey, which tries to avoid the white patch, into a ball that can be lunged at and swallowed in one gulp. The fins emerged close enough to the ship to be touched with a broom handle. I had never seen a wild whale before; even with the writer's loathing of cliché, I must report that it took my breath away.

When the great fin whales sounded, they left behind them on the surface of the ocean pools of smooth water, calm as a garden pond.

Whales have a trick called *spy hopping,* which is basically sticking one's nose above water and having a look around. Whale eyesight is not good, but they see essentially what we would: the outlines of continents, rainbows, ships, gulls, moon, and stars. They see land, sometimes. Whether they remember their ancient lives there is unknowable. That they have no regrets is beyond doubt.

~

What you do to water, you do to the world. Consider this.

How is it that roots, without muscles to squeeze, without a pump to push with, are able to raise water a hundred feet and more from the dirt to the tips of the leaves?

The answer amazes me. The roots do not push; the air pulls. Molecules of water suspended in the air attach themselves to molecules of water at the tips of buds and leaves, and pull, and the molecule they pull pulls the one behind it, and on and on, clear down to the black pools under the earth. Each droplet is joined to each other droplet in a colossal network, a colossal waterwork, a communion of all waters, from the deepest pits to the highest ceiling of the atmosphere. The waters of the abyssal plain link to the water in your brain. The falling rain tugs at the ichor in the body of the worm. A storm over the Pacific stirs your blood. What you do to the puddle in the backyard you do to the world.

~

At the beginning of one September long ago, I bought tropical fish. My friend Kevin Fakhoury sold me an expensive setup for twenty-five dollars, the remnant of an abandoned pet shop business. I filled the tank with neon tetras and peacock-tailed guppies in gold and purple, and four blue-gray ministering bottom cats.

All the catfish are transparent, their guts, the hair-like bones naked to the eye under vivid, taut tissue. When the water is clear they appear to fin about amid nothing, floating in a medium too bright for the ambiance of the room, a seraphic atmosphere dispensing light without itself existing in the ordinary sense of things, a radiant emptiness.

My fish rise to the top of the tank when I approach. My finger pokes through the surface tension until they caress it with their sides or nibble on it with their probing mouths. I know it's greed, but I hope there's a little love, and greed is what love was at the beginning anyway.

By night, their illumination is the red glow of the aquarium heater. They're attracted to this, and one can stand in the dark watching ghostly fish circle that dim radiance like forest creatures at the edge of firelight.

I add two black mollies. A mother guppy gives birth, and two babies survive the ravenings of their tank mates. These hardy remnants bear in them the same elements as I, vomited forth by the same expiring suns. A Martian chemist would find more similarities between me and the guppy than differences. He would know in an instant that we are children of the same womb. Whether the fish realize this or not, they plane their scales to the light, catching and diffusing it like a row of tiny blue moons.

I add sharky scum-suckers, whose Latin name means something like *mouth-on-the-bottom-spiney-one*. A hood is more expense than I can bear, so the water is left open to the air. At morning I find a tetra lying on the carpet. I figure he's been dead for hours, but I dip him in hopefully, and with a jerk that dazzles my hand he's off and away among the plastic kelp. I'd have to work at killing them.

Their ancestors preceded mine and taught them a thing or two. The Field Museum in Chicago has a fossil of a gigantic armored fish, beaked, hooded, terrible, which hails from Cleveland, Ohio, which means it could have swum over the room where I was born, the little house where I grew up, casting its unthinkable shadow on the gleaming sand. I have four limbs because they have two sets of fins.

They swagger over the transplanted white creek rocks. I lower my hand into the tank. If I'm patient, they come to lie between my fingers. I lift them into my world, into the stinging air. Then they're no longer what they were. They're—pardon me—fish out of water. They jump if I keep them in the air too long, their solid, insistent muscle surprising in bodies so small. They are not afraid. They have simply said, *Enough*.

They regard me fairly, dispassionately, but with an understanding of where the advantage lies. I am a blur beyond the glass wall of the world. I am a finger that appears, then disappears, then is followed by a rain of food. But brush that finger with a silken fin, and the food hails down. If I'm run over by a truck tonight, they'll gather in the finger-corner, wondering what went wrong, until the lights go out.

My cousin Diane, pregnant with her first child, walked daily along the shores of the Atlantic. The pregnancy was difficult. She was with her military husband, on assignment far away from everything she had known as a girl, and each day opened a renewed struggle to keep her spirits quick and the child alive. On her beach walks she began collecting black fragments from the sand. Soon she had a box of hard, serrated remembrances. At length someone asked her why she was collecting shark teeth. Though she hadn't really known they were shark teeth, the answer was clear. They were symbols of endurance. She considered the gulfs of time, the abysses of water, the everyday danger they had come through to drift to her feet on the sand. She gathered her shark teeth, and the child was born. Around her neck she wears a black, jagged tooth on a golden chain, where some wear a cross, and for exactly the same reason.

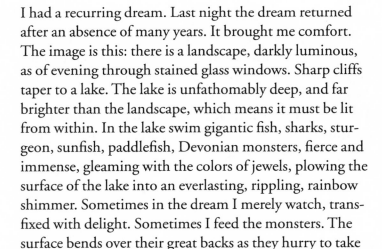

I had a recurring dream. Last night the dream returned after an absence of many years. It brought me comfort. The image is this: there is a landscape, darkly luminous, as of evening through stained glass windows. Sharp cliffs taper to a lake. The lake is unfathomably deep, and far brighter than the landscape, which means it must be lit from within. In the lake swim gigantic fish, sharks, sturgeon, sunfish, paddlefish, Devonian monsters, fierce and immense, gleaming with the colors of jewels, plowing the surface of the lake into an everlasting, rippling, rainbow shimmer. Sometimes in the dream I merely watch, transfixed with delight. Sometimes I feed the monsters. The surface bends over their great backs as they hurry to take food from my hand.

On the night before a certain journey I sleep fitfully, and when I'm finally asleep, I dream vividly. In the dream I travel on an ocean liner. The decks are empty but for me, the atmosphere turbulent with the aftermath—or the heralds—of a storm. I hear commotion to one side of the ship. I lean over the rail, peer into the waters, where white whales sport in the turbulence. I've got McVitties biscuits in my pocket, the ones with chocolate on one side, and I throw them one by one to the whales. When I begin to run out of the biscuits, and the whales begin to lose interest, I assume that the wonders are over, and turn away from the rail. Just then out of the waves come another presence. It is a seal, a golden seal, shining like the sun. It begins to sing.

≈

My friend Holly and I visit the North Carolina Fish Hatchery in the shadow of Looking Glass Mountain. If you buy a quarter's worth of feed, the farm-bred rainbow trout will surface in their cement rivers and suffer you to run your hands down their backs, and along their gleaming sides. A live trout in the water feels—well, not as one expects—soft and hard at once, like wet silk stretched over iron. Phallic. Solid muscle, quick and greedy. A little boy watches us intently. I give him the rest of my feed so he too can lean out over the water and touch the trout. His mother reaches for him, but pulls her hand back. She is uncomfortable, but knows it must be done.

≈

The biota of the soil—amoebae, paramecia, microscopic

vermiforms—are identical to the biota of a pond. The creatures of the earth are aquatic creatures that live in tiny ponds gathered on the surface of particles of soil. This is one of the ten most astonishing facts I know. Does the amoeba that lives in the damp dirt ten feet away from the pond know that it is not living in the pond? Or *is* it living in the pond, water molecule touching water molecule in an inseparable unit only humans or other nonresidents divide up into "pond" and "not-pond"? If I flew to Mars, would I be an earthling anomalously trapped on Mars, or would I have taken the earth with me? Doctor Faustus asks Mephistopheles how he comes to be out of hell, and the demon replies that he is not out of hell, that where he goes, he takes hell with him.

∼

Of the four classical elements, mine is water, not that which stands so much as that which flows. Heraclitean by nature, I peer into roadside ditches as other men peruse the stock reports in the morning paper, and, I guess, for the same reason: for riches, knowledge, power.

Like the Aryan heroes of the Rig-Veda, my task is to make the trapped waters flow.

∼

Saturday morning. I visit the creek in Akron which we patrolled as boys. The houses must have stood just as close then, but we didn't notice; I remember a wide swath of no-man's-land dividing our realm from the ordinary places where we lived the rest of our lives. We were never out of sight of the housewives of East Park, no matter how we shut them from our minds. I've forgotten the old paths, and must thread my way through lots no longer vacant. Once beyond the street, however, all is right. All is as it should have been: the right smells, the right weeds, the right birds in the trees, the right *yiking* of the frogs in amphibian indignation. I remember everything. I remember which flat rocks to lift to find crayfish; I do so, and they are still there, waving their claws curiously against the undersurface of the water. The old forager's excitement quickens my fingers. I lift, probe, poke, bring the lurkers to light.

Finding a good thing so nearly unchanged fills me at first with suspicion, then with gratitude, then with a protectiveness almost wholly useless, considering how far away my life went, how things have been getting along just fine without me. This could have become a subdivision. It could have become a Wal-Mart. For it not to be, even so tentatively, even for this little time, is a wonder and a blessing.

The sameness of the creek after all these years makes me contemplate the varying pace of change. The tempo of our times makes us forget that a thousand generations of our foreparents witnessed nothing new under the sun. There was the murdering blue wall of the glacier. There were the carrion birds thronged at the rim of the forest. The same, sharp, downward chipping motion to flake the same stone scrapers to clean the hides of the same kills.

Now, most of what my father knew—vocationally, anyway—is useless to me. When I was born there were no VCRs, no space vehicles, no Disneyland, no microwave ovens. Computers bulked the size of city blocks; gas was sixteen cents a gallon, and the new interstate system could get us to grandmother's in the next state in hours rather than days.

But the creek flows where it did, where it has for ten thousand years, give or take. If you look on a map of North America, you'll see the Great Lakes at the bottom—which is to say, southern—edge of a system of a zillion or so lakes, some, like Manitoba and the Great Slave, enormous, most of the others too tiny and numerous to be named on the map. These are all gouges and furrows left by the Wisconsin Ice Sheet, that juggernaut of ancient days. Alder Pond, the familiar of my childhood, though not as spectacular as Erie or Superior, is a child of the same mile-high frozen parent, a plunge-pool deep enough and with external sources enough not to disappear with the fathering ice. My creek flows from it into the Little Cuyahoga, and hence into the Cuyahoga and Lake Erie and the Saint Lawrence into the storm-tossed and cod-haunted North Atlantic. So it was when the Egyptians were living in grass huts, when Sumer was a desert yapping with jackals.

Encountering mythology in junior high, I thought of the creek and wondered where its god might dwell, under the rocks, dissolved, diffused through the whole body of the stream, maybe at the deep end where the creek flowed out from the Sullivan Street culvert. At its bottom lay splinters of the Japanese flotillas we launched in imitation of war movies and bombed with stones lobbed from the steep banks. At the bottom lay the bones of kittens Jesse burned to death with sterno from his mother's chafing dish. Somewhere at the bottom, the footprints of Great-Grandmother with her stone scraper, her satchel of magic gleaned from the woods round about.

Frogs are unusual inhabitants of quick, shallow creeks, but ours teemed with them. They were likely washed as tadpoles from Alder Pond. Once adjusted to their new home, they prospered. Leopards as long as your foot let you get close, then leapt six feet easy, stopping your heart in your chest. Bullfrogs blasted in the green pools, heavy as winter boots. You could catch them again and again, for once you were that big there was really nowhere to hide. Their skin was not the green one expected, but barky brown and muddy blue. You can hold them until by their own weight they slide hind-feet first from your hands back into the water.

On the escarpment above the creek was standing water, ponds, which were major breeding grounds of all the local amphibia. Life was tenuous up there at the rim of fields dedicated to a vague but spacious form of industry. Huge areas were scoured and stripped each year by heavy machinery. Our pond may have been an accident of a stuck tire or the idle bite of a steam shovel. But however it got there, it was prodigal—almost *disgusting*—with life, and the major life it boiled with was toads.

One toad species inhabited those parts: rococo-blotched, debonair-ugly *Bufo americanis,* the befriender of gardens, the pest-devourer, he of the hidden riches. The unexpected beauty of the toad's golden eyes led medieval man to speculate that the philosopher's stone, the charm that turns lead into gold, lay cradled in their skulls. Christopher Smart writes in his great, weird masterpiece, *Jubilate Agno:*

> Let Tola bless with the Toad, which is the good
> creature of God,

tho, his virtue is in secret, and his mention is not
made.

Well, I mention him. Toads are certainly the gardener's
ally, devouring slugs and wireworms and every creeping
thing. Their fabled ungainliness disguises a uniform
beneficence, a refreshing state of affairs in a world full
of feints and deceits.

Mary C. Dickerson, in her droll and priceless *The Frog
Book* of 1906, writes, "One-year-old toads are so tame and
confiding that we involuntarily wish them good luck whenever they cross our path." They are and we do. Few non-
mammalian animals look so young when they are young,
or so old when they are old. In the baby toad at the pond's
edge we read limitless potential. In the gnarled veteran of
many summers, lolling plate-wide by the doorstep, we read
a durable wisdom. These views are anthropomorphic, but
not necessarily wrong. Were I to produce the history of
the world as a beast fable, I would cast toads as both up-
start scalawags and Himalayan sages.

In addition to these attainments, they sing. *Bufo americanis* produces a sweet, wavering trill, easily mistaken for
birdsong, until you see the singer. The sound possesses a
subtle bass undertone, as if the toad's inner being, or the
bottom of the pond, or the planet itself, gave back a ghostly
resonation. You can approximate it if you hum very deeply
and whistle at the same time. All North American
Salientia—amphibians that lack tails when mature, e.g.,
frogs and toads—sing. The songs are produced by their
forcing air over vocal cords in the larynx. Unlike the
grunting of fish and the clicking of mollusks, these are
true voices—in fact, the Ur-voice of Gaea, upon which

the nightingale and Kiri Te Kanawa are variations. The first voice lifted over the waters was amphibian.

Toads, though they seek dampness under stones, in cellars, in the cool of forests, do not drink in the ordinary way. Necessary moisture is absorbed through the skin.

To absorb rather than gulp down seems to me a particular grace, akin to the immaculate consumption by plants of pure sunlight.

The habits of the toad are ethereal, to compensate for the earthiness of his aspect. He destroys the ravagers, slugs, cutworms, crop-devouring caterpillars. He swallows with his eyes.

Gideon, marching against the Midianites, divides his host into those that bend over and lap water like a dog, and those that bring the water to their mouths with their hands. The Lord does not command him according to those who sprawl in the shallows and absorb. Thus is the toad kept at peace.

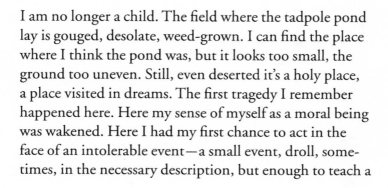

I am no longer a child. The field where the tadpole pond lay is gouged, desolate, weed-grown. I can find the place where I think the pond was, but it looks too small, the ground too uneven. Still, even deserted it's a holy place, a place visited in dreams. The first tragedy I remember happened here. Here my sense of myself as a moral being was wakened. Here I had my first chance to act in the face of an intolerable event—a small event, droll, sometimes, in the necessary description, but enough to teach a small boy that it is possible to act in the face of numbing atrocity.

Why I remember it was Good Friday is unclear, but I do remember, and that my friend Jack Herald and I had taken our school day off to fish in the creek. "Fish," as I have said, is a misleading term, meaning in this context to comb the creek bed for nymphs, hideous larvae, crustaceans, amphibia—everything, in fact, but fish, which were far too fast, and clung to the deeper pools.

We did not keep what we caught. Part of this was a conscious effort to balance our friend Jesse, who hauled considerable biomass up from the creek to toss onto his garage roof to die and decay, thus to add to his smelly but impressive collection of skeletons. Centerpieces of his collection were a dog and a cat and what he claimed was an opossum, though under that corruption it could have been anything. Part of our abstinence was, however, a genuine ecological bent, which, now that I think of it, seems to have been self-generated. Perhaps it would be more correct to call it a form of natural religion. It was a desecration, except under extraordinary circumstances, to do anything other than find it, look at it, drop it back into the water.

We worked our way up to the deep end, from which the next logical step was the tadpole pond on the heights. There we found horror. Big boys, teenagers we didn't know, had invaded our pond. Now that I think of it, it was probably *their* pond, as it lay much closer to the Sullivan Street–Newton Street neighborhoods than it did to us way up on Goodview Avenue. But if it was theirs, they were treating it in a way we never dreamed. It was spring, and tens of dozens of toads had come to mate and lay their ropes of eggs. The strange boys were standing knee-deep in the toads' warm water, lifting up the mating pairs and whacking them skyward with baseball bats. The toads exploded midair, paying out gut and semicircles of pale blood. Some of the boys were throwing toads onto the bank, where others shot them with air rifles jammed down their gullets, or set them sailing with bats swung like golf clubs.

A toad in agony excretes a poisonous liquid from its head; if you are a dog with a toad in your mouth, this is quite convincing. Against air rifles and baseball bats, even hands, it has no effect whatever.

I recall two emotions from those first terrifying seconds. The first and more powerful was the conviction that it must be an illusion, or some prank staged by the teenagers to frighten us. Nothing at once so horrible and so pointless could *really* be happening. The second emotion was cunning. I was angry, but I knew that my anger had to meet superior force. I shouted something which could be taken for glee, ran to the pond and let the boys think that I thought what they were doing was wonderful, and I wanted to do it too. They seemed agreeable. At least they let me into the pond. They let me begin gathering toads. I pitched a few over the hill into the woods. This had to be done in such a way as to make it look like I was *throwing* them rather than saving them. Those that didn't make it clear into the trees I nudged over the slope with my toe. This was a mistake. I'd saved maybe twenty in this wise until the boys caught on and saw that I was a false toad tormentor. They came at *me* with their bats and air rifles. I knew the time for subtlety was over.

I yelled, *"Now!"* at Jack, as though we had a plan worked

out all along and were just waiting for a signal. He watched me while I jammed toads into my pockets, under my shirt, anywhere they could be carried. When there was no toad space left, I began to run. I couldn't understand why it was so important to the boys that they have *all* the toads, but it was, and they ran after me. Under my shirt, the toad lovers still locked thigh to thigh, rutting and chirring against my skin. The damp and the sticky against my skin must be— no, it was too horrible to think about. Part of the energy of my escape was disgust at their carnality, the sickening purity of obsession that respected neither my sacrifice nor their own safety.

Like Hippolytus running before Atalanta, I tossed toads to one side or the other as the boys closed in, hoping some-how to save the remnant. I heard the sound of small bod-ies squashing under boots behind me. The boys didn't catch me. They must have given up, for I was small and slow and could never have outrun them. I pulled seven toads from under my shirt and set them on the dry leaves of the forest floor, where they would be safe. They kept on rutting, though the eggs they laid in that desert were lost. I remember *seven,* a number held against a day of atonement.

They caught Jack and killed his toads. They hit him in the belly hard enough to smash their backs without hurt-ing him that much. He ran home, wailing, his shirt wring-ing blood that I thought at first was his.

In my complex history as a sleeper, I've had three or four re-curring dreams, all of them beautiful. One of them involves the tadpole pond, which despite that Good Friday long ago, brings peace with its return. In the dream, a forbidding wilderness engulfs the scraggly urban wilderness of my boyhood. Sometimes the main barrier is a desert, more often a swamp or steep escarpments, or a plain of clinging, impenetrable vines, which I laboriously negotiate, longing to get beyond them, to what I am never sure. Though these barriers are deadly, they are also very beautiful, and I move through my labors without resentment, but with a hushed solemnity. Finally, in the twilight of the dream, I gain the circle of crags amid which lies The Water. Though this water is the tadpole pond of my boyhood, no one would recognize it as such but me. It has sunk into the caldera of a mountain, a lake, a shimmering mirror, radiant, holy, all but inaccessible. I lean over the crags to look. The body of the water lies immense and incalculably deep, gleaming cobalt blue, as though lit from beneath and within. Great creatures ply the water, sharks, rays, maned eels, sunfish, beasts of every shape and every hue of the rainbow, all like the falling of light through the windows of a cathedral, in ruby and topaz, cerulean, violet, burgundy and gold, orange, velvet black. In the quiet of evening, the waters churn silently with their myriads of burning life.

I hold off waking. I look, and look.

Walkers

Τ HE VERNAL EQUINOX. It is at once the last day of winter and the first day of spring. I've driven north up the Blue Ridge Parkway to the seasonal barrier at Craggy Garden. The barrier says, BEYOND THIS POINT, SNOW. I exit the car, fuss with my gear, put on an extra shirt, start walking. Beyond the barrier, the Craggy Pinnacle Tunnel remains impassable. Breast-shaped mounds of ice block the driving lanes, drippage from the ceiling made into incipient glaciers. I run through the tunnel, because it is so cold. I entered at the south, and when I run at last through the north entrance, I break through a wall of light, like a high school football player through a paper gate. It must have been this bright on the other side, but I did not notice. I keep trotting, to get as deep into the light as I can. It is blue, of course, but the word does not quite suffice. Living blue. Crystalline. I slow, gradually; the light is a palpable substance, dragging on my cuffs and sleeves. Snow lies in ravines and on the northern faces of the mountains. Snow-colored clouds marble the horizons. I am walking in a sapphire whose few snowy imperfections intensify the universal light.

Except for the prongs of distant mountains, I walk atop everything visible. If I sailed off the road, I would hit nothing until I slammed into the Rockies or the Pyrenees. A raven flaps over the valley, beating fast for so large a bird, chattering to himself like a sorcerer rehearsing spells. I am walking a blue crystal, utterly alone.

It was a mistake to articulate those words, "utterly alone," for as I do, a frisson made half of terror and half of delight flashes through my system. I could keel over, and the raven would be the first to find me, maybe by a margin of days. But it is not that, really, which shakes me. It is the idea that I came here knowing I would be alone, counting on it, desiring it, lying to people who asked where I was going, so that I might be imperially alone.

What is wrong with me? I ask the echoing face of Craggy Dome. If it has an opinion, it does not share it. I walk for two or three hours. I nap for half an hour on a sunny, south-facing bank, secure that nobody will see me. The raven will. He'll be watching to see if I move, if I twitch, if there are signs of breathing. I walk back to the car in just over an hour, a veritable beeline compared to my meandering outward journey. It is a feast, an orgy of solitude, and I gobble it down, with the orgiast's greed, and shame.

When I get back through the tunnel, three boys are bellowing at and jostling each other on the breasts of ice, sliding, trying to clamber to the top long enough to have their pictures taken. I want to ask them if they want me to take a shot of all three of them together, but somehow I don't; somehow I creep past them, not more than ten feet away from the nearest, as quietly, as beast-like as I can

manage. I am not sure whether they have seen me or not
until I get to the car and slam the door behind me. They
all jump and look toward me. I passed through their midst
on my little beast feet, undetected. I want to feel triumphant, want to congratulate myself on a feat of woodcraft. But instead, I am horrified. I am invisible to my
own. At one point, I must have wanted this.

Long ago I acquired the habit of hiking alone. It arose
originally from being a sickly child. The embarrassment
of not being able to keep up was mitigated by not having
anybody to keep up with. But when the sickliness was left
behind, the habit of solitude was not. Another person on
the trail distracts me. Meeting someone in the woods, one
smiles and says, "Hey," but one considers turning back,
one considers calling it a day, because one knows the trail
ahead contains none of the surprises available to the first
soul passing. Like a Castilian husband, the walker prizes
virginity.

    If the other person is *with* me, the distraction multi-
plies. I don't imply an unpleasant distraction. Few experiences are not improved by sharing, just different, just not
what I am usually looking for in a jaunt to the wild, an
encounter with a soul rather than a Soul. Fine.

    But sometimes you leave before first light, tiptoeing
in the dark, trying not to bang into things, carrying your
shoes to lace them on the doorstep, your companion still
sleeping, or maybe wide awake, conspiring with you,
knowing what you need today.

    Here is a memory of a walk when I was a child: I am
very small, and sensible of the need to keep to the path, as

otherwise I would be lost in the undergrowth which waves above my head as surely as the trees. A man walks in front of me. I think he is my father, though the picture is unclear, and when I mentioned this to him, he had no memory of it. The man speaks. I don't understand the words, and for a while suppose he's jabbering on in the unfathomable way adults have. Suddenly I realize he's giving names to the trees. Oak. Maple. Dogwood. I run up close to him, so as to miss nothing. *Dogwood? Why that?* I wonder without asking. I'm afraid to say anything, to make any response, lest the flow of naming stop. The man is much taller than I. I follow him out of the trees and toward a patch of sun. It doesn't occur to me that I have any other choice, though I long to turn back, long to reenter the room full of spirits which have just been given names, and thus lives.

Great lovers know something that merely obsessive lovers do not understand. In the highest love there is communion, but never identity. The perfect union of lovers is the end of love. The soul is always singular.

It is second or third grade. Mrs. Timberlake leads us through the great south meadow of the city park. She teaches kindergarten, and she walks to school, and each day draws a gaggle of the neighborhood children with her to school in her wake. I keep trying to join the throng, but they go too fast, and it is impossible for me to keep up. I try to run in little spurts, but I slow after a few yards, like a toy winding down. For a few seconds I am mortally afraid. I want to cry out to them to come back and get me, but mortification outranks fear, and instead I sink down into the long grass, where they would have a hard time finding me even if they wanted to. I don't know that I'm sick. I think I'm lazy, or not made right in some way, or that they have been given some charm of fleetness arbitrarily denied to me. I sink deeper into the grass, lying on my back, looking up where the plants are a green and tawny and golden fringe, the sky a blue tent above them. It is safe and enclosed. It is very beautiful. I focus on a stalk of grass at eye level, where at that exact moment a praying mantis arranges herself for a better look at me. It is spring, and she is quite small. Dainty. I know enough not to touch her. Her sawtooth arms brace against a neighboring blade, her head turns to keep me in focus, like a farmer leaning on a fence to get a better look at the two-headed calf.

She is witnessing the birth of a naturalist.

Same field, two years later. Mrs. Timberlake no longer walks to school, so everyone walks by themselves. We're supposed to keep to the Newton Street sidewalk, but we cut across the meadow because it's quick, beautiful, and forbidden. It is also dangerous. We see Lonnie Banks coming a long way off. He is the school bully, older than we and twice our size, though in the same grade. He has told us not to walk the meadow, claiming it as personal property, a claim strengthened by the yellow sash of SCHOOL PATROL he wears perpetually across his shoulder. We are officially not allowed to use the meadow to come to school (though it is a city park, and *it* doesn't mind), and Steve has Rule to back his tyranny. He leaps from the woods edge when he sees us coming, like a young ram defending his turf. We scan for an adult whose protection we can put ourselves under, but there is none. Steve is furlongs away yet, so my pals take the main chance and begin to run. With a head start, they'll probably be safe. I can't run. I plod on, conserving my energy. Steve pulls up beside me, panting and red in the face. He says, "I told you not to."

I keep plodding.

He says, "I want you to go all the way back and stay on the street."

In some ways it's a perfectly legitimate request. The principal told him to say this to the transgressors he caught. But I keep plodding, with my eyes thrown to one side, in order to watch his every move. His fist comes down on my shoulder. It came too fast, and I really didn't know what to do to stop it. I see him raise his arm to hit me again. I turn, fast as a dog myself, land two blows on his stomach and one on the very tip of his nose. He grabs the nose, with blood running between his fingers. It is not enough that he stands there, looking flabbergasted, trying to decide whether to hold his stomach or his nose. I want more from the incident. I launch at him again, this time screaming. Before I can get to him, he turns and runs. I chase him until I'm out of breath, feeling an exhilaration I cannot quite define.

Steve is standing at the edge of the sassafras grove, watching me. He has witnessed the birth of a fighter.

∼

I hike Graveyard Fields in the blazing light, feeling health and strength in every corpuscle. I walk up the center of the cold river, glad for the sturdiness of my sneakers, glad for the trout darting away from my shadow. Butterflies accept my back and shoulders as a sort of lumpy island midstream. My feet tingle in the cold water, massaged, wanting more. We are told that rubies are dug out of the mountain by this river, so I let my eyes rest on anything that gives off a dim gleam of red. Beauty around me. Beauty over me. Beauty under and against me. The naming of beauty becomes a sort of prayer, a mantra urging me forward in the sparkling water. I take white stones from the stream to place in my aquarium, to remember the day by. I am happy. I know where I'm going, this being the second time I have hiked Graveyard Fields.

The first time was when my friend Kit ventured down from his veterinary practice in New York for a visit. In college he was the strongest man I knew for his size, a varsity wrestler, a marathon runner, not large, but wiry, handsome, seemingly inexhaustible. In graduate school he widened his interests, becoming a potter, a musician, a poet, an expert in those things which require shaping and patient consideration. Though we never lost touch, there were often years between our meetings. This didn't bother me, as I assumed we had all the time in the world to make it up.

The world seldom forgives such presumption.

Kit fades month by month from multiple sclerosis. No longer able to wrestle horses or lift calves, he has had to turn to housecats in order to remain in veterinary practice. His marriage to a bitter and selfish woman has had predictable results, and he finds himself not only disabled, but abandoned. Insomnia and depression keep him staring at the ceiling through the endless nights. His visit is not a particularly happy occasion. I make myself awkward wondering what to do to make him feel comfortable. He came to me sad and sick, and I am at a loss as to how to act, what to say, until I begin to see in him the old mirth and defiance. It is all right. He is the same person. Only his body has changed.

We manage to go hiking at Graveyard Fields. Every step or two I ask, "Are you all right?" until he tells me to shut the hell up.

We pick up a path of blood at the very edge of the parking lot. We follow it down the forest path, the blood here thickening where the hunter set its quarry down, there thinning to droplets when the hunter ran. The path crosses the Pigeon River at a cluster of deep, clear pools, and in one pool floats a slurry of blood where the creature paused to nibble its prize. A blood-swollen organ turns over and over in the flowing water, immaculate from the scouring of the current. I touch it before I realize what it is. At my touch, it bursts into a scarlet cloud. Kit thinks it might be a spleen. It seems quite large. We imagine the loping carnivore capable of killing the owner of such an organ. The forest carries the unmistakable tang of fox. This is the likely hunter, though who the victim was we never discover. Perhaps a roadkill hauled down from the parkway. There are bobcats in Graveyard Fields. We prayed for one of them to be involved. Perhaps a bear, though a creature that size would have left prints even in the scant earth of the trail.

On that day I felt insolently vigorous. I was showing off, more than a little. Kit had always been the athlete.

Without awareness of how mean the victory was, I relished climbing where he could no longer climb, lifting what he could no longer lift, running when he had to put his hand on his knee and lean painfully into the slope. I was not being intentionally cruel. I don't know that he noticed, or that I would have if I hadn't written it down; the documented life is never innocent.

I cavorted on the edge of the waterfall, effervescent, feeling perhaps that I could lighten him a little with my lightness. I bellowed highlights of the Steeleye Span album that had been our mutual favorite years before. I tried to gazelle-leap between two boulders. No gazelle, I slipped backward into the water, on down the slope of the polished rocks, not afraid, really, until I sensed that I could not catch myself. The rocks were slippery, the current cold and deep and very strong. There the river plunges sixty feet onto tumbled boulders, plunges again, finally three times to the valley floor. I was falling. I was going to die. It was, aside from everything else, embarrassing.

What happened was at that moment, Kit put forth all the speed that was in him, ran, grabbed my arm, pulled me back from the center of the current to where I could reach his body, and then the rocks. The grip of his hand on my arm was tremendous, a god's grip, tranquil and unbreakable.

On the path climbing back to the parking lot, I say, "You still have it."

He answers, "No, you've *got* it. I just needed it one last time."

Kurt, who is not curt at all, but the tallest person I know, pauses over a cluster of ant hills bathed in brilliant light. The sun is admitted into the forest by a fallen beech, but how the sand got there I don't know. Maybe the ants hauled it up from the guts of the mountain, as they sometimes do fossils and arrowheads. Kurt stands stock still, contemplating. Finally, with his toe he nicks the top of the anthill, sending a cascade of sand down into the hole.

I say, "What are you doing?"

"History. I'm making history. I want them to remember today."

We kick in two of the dozen or so anthills, to obtain the randomness of a real event. As we walk, we imagine the chronicles by which the scribes of the Myrmidons will memorialize our passing.

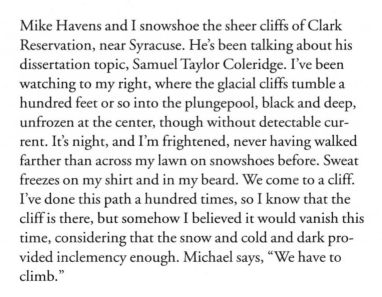

Mike Havens and I snowshoe the sheer cliffs of Clark Reservation, near Syracuse. He's been talking about his dissertation topic, Samuel Taylor Coleridge. I've been watching to my right, where the glacial cliffs tumble a hundred feet or so into the plungepool, black and deep, unfrozen at the center, though without detectable current. It's night, and I'm frightened, never having walked farther than across my lawn on snowshoes before. Sweat freezes on my shirt and in my beard. We come to a cliff. I've done this path a hundred times, so I know that the cliff is there, but somehow I believed it would vanish this time, considering that the snow and cold and dark provided inclemency enough. Michael says, "We have to climb."

"That's a lousy idea."

"Then we'll have to go back the way we came."

I'm so tired I can't help him make the decision. I think of the narrow rock path meandering the cliff edge. I think of the star-filled void above the freezing water. I think of my propensity to tread on my own snowshoes and pitch sideways.

We climb the cliff. How we let it get so dark I don't know. I'm cursing under my breath, blaspheming every fingerhold, every agonizing straddle around the clownish shoes. Mike remains silent, his way of expressing the same thing.

At the top, pouring sweat, breathless, we begin to run, legs spread like those of animals three times taller than we are. We've said nothing to each other, never made a sign. Anything to put that cliff behind us. We do not say anything until we get back to the car, knock our snowy shoes against the ground, climb wearily in, head for home. I say nothing because I am speechless with fury. Against Michael? I don't know. Against the night and the cold? Surely. It is a long time before I go out in it again.

It is, finally, best to go alone. At the least, I drive my companions berserk with stopping and poking and flipping over stones.

≈

In college came the Year of the Female Hiking Companion.

Jane was good for long hauls over hills, through bogs, into the dangers of the local farms with their dogs and wild-running, evil-tempered sows. Jane skipped class to hike with you and expected the same in return.

Toni decided to take up hiking as a cure for a dramatic case of panphobia, the fear of everything. I'm trying to think of something in the outside which she didn't fear. One was willing to be part of the therapy for a while, until—after the umpteenth dog barked or pheasant exploded underfoot or other hiker appeared unanticipated and set Toni screaming at prodigious pitch and duration, hands pressed over her ears so she wouldn't have to hear herself—one thought again of the pleasures of solitude.

Heather was the best of the lot. She could make a pun out of the name or attributes of any woodland creature. Gaudy birds—kingfishers, green herons, sun-struck warblers—gathered themselves until the moment her binoculars were raised. She homed in on salamander rocks with a hunter's sureness. With her unhurried doe-gait, Heather was tireless, ever ready for the next rise, the next turn of the path. It is a comfort in this changeable world that every year or so, Heather and I get together and hike again, in more exotic settings, wearier and slower, but with the same sense of limitless expectancy.

Hiking is, however, except under special circumstances, a single-sex activity. Women are better off hiking with women, men with men. Men, for perfectly justified evolutionary reasons, get protective and show-offy around women in the wild. We turn from doctors and cellists into bull bison, huffing and flaring our nostrils, hacking at innocent vegetation, making elaborate plans to meet the least likely hazards. Women who remain calm and uncomplaining on the trail can be a provocation to the male, who secretly longs for some calamity by which his courage and woodcraft can be put on display. Women carry civilization with them, even on the trail. Men atavize. Men forget the polyresins swathing our bodies, the hum of traffic on the Parkway sixty yards away. Our ears cock for the stirring of panthers, the tread of enemy moccasins. We are always playing army against the day when we really go to war, always playing space adventurer against the day when lives really do depend on the skill with which we meet unforeseeable circumstance. Women know everything is a game with us; sometimes they need to be reminded why.

A friend maintains that the one irreducible social, psychological, and functional difference between men and women is that men like to piss in the woods—prefer it, even—and women do not. I have considered this notion, and it seems sound. No matter how enlightened in other matters, we men feel that the ease of our micturition is somehow a mark of superiority. For men hiking together this issue is not noticed; nor, I imagine, is it when women hike together. But when men and women mix, a voice at the back of his mind wonders every mile or so, "When will she have to do it?" alternately relishing and dreading the opportunity to stop, to wait, to heave great and patient sighs while she goes about her business.

The same friend, mentioned above, continues to speculate that the difference in wilderness bathroom capability is proof that civilization was created by women. I buy this, too. The reason that the intelligent porpoise doesn't *achieve* anything is that he is too comfortable doing that which comes naturally. Surely the human male was in the same situation, hunting with his buddies, pissing luxuriously, barely breaking stride, trailing home with the meat over his shoulder, planning new ways to brag about it all. Woman, on the other hand, was never comfortable. She nagged until somebody built her *a room,* then lined it with tiles, maybe installed a fresco of leaping porpoises, put in plumbing. Presto: civilization.

~~~

Accepting a hiking buddy is as particular and personal as choosing a career or a mate, and informs you as much about yourself. It tells you what you need from someone when it will be but you and he against the world. Sometimes it's enough that he'll carry half the gear, or that he has a stove that weighs nothing and tans you at fifty paces. Sometimes it's much subtler, much more vital and inexpressible.

I had a perfect hiking buddy once. Of course Rob carried his half, but it went way beyond that. He didn't mention it when I wadded the maps instead of folding them with the hermetic precision affected by some outdoorsy types. He didn't exhaust one telling of past adventures in the wildwood. He didn't know so much that you couldn't tell him a thing or two. Or, as I suspect, he knew plenty, but didn't mind hearing it again from a different source. Rob was especially suited to a blabbermouth like me because, though he was an expert camper, he was zero as a naturalist, and I could inform, inform, inform, and he had the grace to affect to find it all amazing. He could hold his liquor no better than I, and when we were so ill-advised as to drink heavily after a long day hiking, we would both find everything we saw miraculous, memorable, worth re-hashing over and over, as long as we stayed awake.

He was also a Buddhist, which is something I admire, but which lies still far from my hasty and discursive nature. I would say, "The frogs are early this year," and he would reply, "The frogs are always on time." I would be trudging to the campground laundry room, and see through the trees, fluttering, a sharp-shinned hawk, striped tail dragging like a spear in the air behind. I'd look around quick to find Rob so he could see too, and there he would be, laundry bag dropped to the ground, his hands folded in that Buddha-gesture of homage and compassion.

I wanted to introduce the creatures of the woods to him. I wanted them to like each other. I pull a log out of the muck near a woodland creek, hoping to find a salamander. I do, a lovely green-gold one, the color of an old coin or an autumn leaf. I hold it up to Rob, cupping my hand the way you must, half way between crushing and escape. He shrinks back. I think he must believe it's a snake. I say, amazed at the reaction, "It's a *salamander.*"

"Doesn't it bite?"

I touch the creature's nose with the tip of my finger. "You see it doesn't."

I push the salamander at him until he takes it in his hand, still uneasy. I say "OK," and take it back. His shoulders sag with relief. I say, "Didn't you ever play with salamanders when you were little?"

"No. Gators. Looks like a gator to me."

We have the standard lecture on the difference between reptiles and amphibians. The whole while, the 'mander rests in my palm, which I open more and more as the creature grows calm. How cold it is, how small, its claws, though I feel them, exquisite to the point of invisibility. I don't understand how anything so small and cold

can live. I don't understand how anything so small can
scare anybody, but it has scared Rob, and I file that away,
not as something odd nor as a weakness, but as something
rather lovely, like a red spot in a yellow rose, a Lab that
hesitates before the water.

Prionosuchus plummeri roamed the Brazilian river bottoms 230 million years ago. Thirty feet long, with the ta-
pering needle jaws of a crocodile, it was the largest land
animal and most formidable predator of the Permian Age.
Also, it was an amphibian, the father, or at least the wicked
uncle, of the salamanders. I stood there cradling the specter
of those terrible genes in my hand, a creature two inches
long, whose skull I could crush with a flick of my hand.
Rob may not be foolish at all; he may simply have a longer
memory.

Rob and I make a pilgrimage to Joyce Kilmer Memorial
Forest, at the western tip of North Carolina. We drive
through mountains darkened with storm and scurrying
cloud, dazzled with zigzags of light. We've gone there because it is one of the few stands of mountain vegetation
not bulldozed by the glaciers, a forest ecosystem continu-
ous beyond anything else above the tropics. The old
woman in the parking lot, she with the anemone in her
buttonhole, the guardian, ancient dryad, tells us that we
will find the largest hemlock in the world. What we do
surely find is a land perhaps *too* alive, too redolent with the
breath of trees. The air is so moist as to be visible. The
lungs pull at their own corners, trying to get bigger. It is
like finding yourself sealed in a terrarium.

It is the richest forest I have ever seen: life upon life,

root under root, ply over ply, golden toadstools gnawed
by black-and-gold beetles, snow-colored anemone backed
by trunks of lustrous, absolute black, the red of broken
hemlock, the silver of mist, silver flashes of braided creeks
in the understory, orange and pale of fungus, rust-backed
toads, gigantic millipedes of elegant dust-rose and pewter,
blood-red wake-robin, over all, of course, green, green,
and green. Dazzling green. Electric green. Moss green.
Shadowy viridian. Emerald. Jade. Mist green. Sea green.
Hemlock silver-green. Gold-green of the tulip-poplars
diffusing down from two hundred feet above our heads.

It is almost incredible that I notice another color amid
those colors, but I do, and whisper to Rob, "Behind you."

A Blackburnian warbler harvests the path's edge at our
feet. Rob stands, a latter-day Moses, awestruck by the
Burning Bird. The warbler, not similarly impressed, takes
its sweet time. We grow impatient, and brush past the
gleaning bird, he yielding the path just enough for the
seams of our jeans to pass him by.

Rob says, "I didn't know birds were so *different.*" Such
a comment would sound ignorant if I didn't know what
he meant. He goes—or at least went, until he met me—to
the wildwood to get away from things, to close his eyes into
the mist of *nothing in particular,* to rest. I go to the wildwood in order to enter the storm of the particular, to name
the names of *things,* to be about my proper business.

We exhaust each other. After a day together we can collapse against tree roots, against cold boulders in a beating
hail, sleep anywhere.

Rob says, "You're different in the woods." I accept that
as a statement of fact, until I consider that he's almost

never known me elsewhere. He must be right, though;
we all are.

⌇

Holly and I hike in the shadow of Mount Pisgah one
morning late in winter. We come across a purple knit hat
stuck onto a twig. I know the hat is Rob's. I know that he
has left it there on purpose. I smell his smell on it, at once
comforting and lonely, though whether the loneliness is
his or mine I don't know. I should think first of danger,
that he may be lost or hurt in the woods, but it doesn't
seem very likely.

Holly says, "Somebody you know?"

Inexplicably I answer, "No."

A mile or so farther on, I take off my hat, put on his. I
give my hat to Holly. The circle stands complete.

Scavengers

THE LEASE SAYS SO CLEARLY, "No children," that
when I hear the screaming in the parking lot I think I
should complain. Not screaming, really: laughing, talking
in the low voices of childhood conspiracy. The small ones
cry when they tumble onto the pavement. I look through
the slats of the blinds at them. They all seem to ride small
plastic vehicles with uneven plastic wheels that make
noise on the cement like a heavy tropical rain on a tin
roof. The youngest is a boy with a white tricycle. His father rides with him sometimes. He's a photographer for
the city paper, with that raggedy, unkempt handsomeness
that cameramen and drummers share. He rides his ten-
speed around his son on his trike for the entire weekend,
swiveling and banking so the boy is never out of sight.
When I go outside, the father says, "You should try this
sometime," though whether he means riding a bike
around in a parking lot, or having a son, I'm not sure.

The rest of the resident (and illicit) children are girls.
Two, on the brink of adolescence, seem able to roller skate
all day, down stairs, up stairs, across flats and lawns and
places where I am hard put to walk. I know there's some

skill subtler than skating afoot here, but when I watch them to find out exactly what, they turn coy and fade into the doors of their own townhouses. They make up games that involve stealth and reconnaissance. They reach through mail slots and open doors with their skinny arms when you have locked yourself out—positively love doing that, in fact. When they're out in the midst of one of their intricate games, I take too long to open my door, walk too slowly to my car, so as to take in as much as possible. But they're on to me. They keep their secrets.

One is fat and loud; one is slender and loud and very beautiful. I don't know which to pity more for what will come. A third girl is younger and smaller, and the loveliest of the lot. Her red hair flies behind her as she hurries to keep up with the other girls. Like the tail of some dinosaurs, the hair possesses a separate consciousness, wild, nervous, devoid of the inhibitions that mediate the actions of the body. She's smarter than the older girls, smarter than most of the people she will ever meet. I talked with her in the laundromat once, and if I closed my eyes and deepened her voice I wouldn't have known her from a woman of some poise. She knows when to speak in complete sentences and when not. She doesn't seem to care that the older girls ignore her. She watches, studies, mimics whatever they do better than they did it; her relationship to them is that of a reader to her books: use without engagement.

When I first moved here she had an older brother whom she adored. It was funny to watch her follow him, doubling his gestures like a tiny red shadow. He was a teenager, but, like her, small for his age, a wise child bandaged at every corner from precipitous descents from skateboards. He's gone now, maybe living with his father. I make up stories in which he returns in a long white limo and takes his little sister wherever she thinks about when she skates alone in the red hour before night.

Older children have dances in the clubhouse above my window. It's hard to see, but very easy to hear them. When I do see them, they look like most kids, skinny and funny, wearing oversized shirts in the bright teal that's fashionable now. The lease says so clearly, "No children," that when I have to shut my blinds so they can't look directly into my bedroom, I think I should complain. But I ask myself, "Does it really bother you?" and the answer is, *No.* I stand on my side of the blinds, listening, trying to hear what they laugh at when they laugh. My stealth, their freedom when unobserved, their skittishness under observation, even the word "blind" invests the event with the feel of natural observation. Add this one to the life list. Mark *that* behavior, never before seen.

Two or three times a summer, somebody's exhausted parents send a party of them on a scavenger hunt. I think these parties have something to do with church, for the children are scrubbed and combed, and look like their parents would have on such an occasion a quarter of a century ago. I hear their voices outside my door, conferring as to whether they should bother somebody they don't know. The answer is, of course, *No,* but I am hoping they are not altogether so sedate as they appear; I am hoping that they ring the bell and ask for green thread and black buttons and matchbooks from restaurants in other states. I watch their faces as they ask, trying to fathom what they are thinking, trying to remember what I would have thought myself a quarter of a century ago. They think I am from another planet. I stand and listen as they explain, in loud, simple words, what a scavenger hunt is, and that they mean me no harm. I scurry around, finding what I have, bringing some of the wrong things, to see if they'll take them. When they're gone, I leave my porch light on, so the next team will know I am home and maybe have some green thread left.

When I leave the house late that night, I drag my hand across the shrub in front. I have snagged something. I pull my hand back, dragging with it from the damp leaf a single green thread.

A gray kitten—of the kind which in the natural course of things must be called Smoky—came to my door. I put a bowl of milk in the grass beside my door, for the kitten, of course, but when I came home that night and switched on the light, something brownish was floating in the liquid, which seemed otherwise untouched. The brown things proved to be the tangled bodies of slugs that had crawled into the milk. The sides of the bowl and the ground around gleamed with the sliding chocolate masses of them. I overturned the bowl with my toe, unable to account for the feeling of revulsion. It was as though the kitten had turned into them, an absurd idea, of course, but once it got into my head, it wouldn't be gone. I got my sack of sea-salt and sprinkled them all, watching while they writhed and sloughed their skins as though scalded by blasts of steam. Nor was I content with that one slaughter. Night after night I snapped on the porch light, quickly, as though they were rabbits to scurry away when they saw me coming. I watched for the brown lumps on the stone step, for the telltale gleam from the blades of grass. I sifted out salt from my bag onto their backs, watched them wither and die. If someone asked, I would say, "They destroy vegetation, you know," but that wasn't the real motivation. What the real motivation was I can't imagine. One night I'm hunting in the grass, backing through the dewy blades, and I feel a tickle on the back of my hand. I do not reflexively flick it off. If it's a slug, I'll want to annihilate it, as I have been doing all the rest. I turn the hand over slowly and look at what's on the back of it. The shape is bigger, darker than I expected. It is a black widow spider. I flick then, believe me. I go inside, done with the slaughter of the slugs, that night and forever.

Spring

MARCH. The Blue Ridge Parkway has been closed for weeks, because of ice storms followed by gale-force winds which shattered the trees and sent limbs and trunks crashing down so that the road and most of the forest paths lie impassable. On foot, though, one can laboriously make one's way. I climb over hulks of tulip-poplars, shredded like kindling, over tangles of laurel uprooted like pulled weeds. It takes me seven hours to go as far as I could go in four last fall. On each side of me, six-foot branches are driven into the ground like javelins. To have been in the forest when the wind came on the tail of ice would have been to die. Or so I say, dramatically, finding nary a corpse amid the kindling.

I've hiked longer than I expected, and am tired. Not one other human figure moved across the mountain at any time, though the day is blue and cool, perfect for hiking. People probably checked with the Forest Service and were told, "The Parkway is closed," and believed it. The highway is deserted and strewn with twisted lumber. Shadows grow long. The moon climbs behind the blue range eastward, still invisible, waiting to peek out in half

an hour and take the mountains back from the realm of
Night. I break from the cover of the forest and walk maybe
fifteen paces before stopping dead. A skunk forages on the
roadside, not more than a running long jump away. It's a
large male, creamy white in two thick bands along his
back, black only in a narrow stripe down the center, so
pale that I'm not sure he's a skunk until he faces me with
that unmistakable sad clown mask. We regard each other
a long time. I'm downward of a considerable wind, and
his vision is worse than mine. When I tire of waiting I
shout, "Skunk! It's just me! Let me pass!" so he'll know
what I am and that my intentions are obvious enough to
be honorable. Surprising a skunk is, after all, a very bad
idea. He swivels to keep his beady eye on me, but continues foraging. I edge by, knowing who is the master of this
situation.

Skunks are Mustelidae, a family including weasels,
fishers, otters, ferrets, badgers, and that Shiva-beast, the
wolverine. The skunk is one of the three or four most familiar wild animals in North America, and yet certain
things about it remain almost unknown. First, like us, it
does not stink if it is happy. Second, it is a serene creature,
perturbable only by the most extreme provocation. Third,
it sings.

It was another March, long ago, when I first heard a
skunk sing. I walked by starlight down Udall Road in
Hiram, Ohio, when I heard her in a field between me
and the valley forest. I watched her waddle from the
shadow of the trees, to the road, across the road, not more
than six feet away, the whole while mumbling and twittering to herself like someone deep in thought.

Central to the experience was the odd sense of having

encountered her before—not just some skunk, but *her*.
Something in her lack of either skittishness or aggression
let me assume a shared memory of acceptance. The next
day, wanting that intensity of experience again, I skipped
class and fought through the encircling brambles into the
valley of Silver Creek. I moved north on the high ridge
between Udall Road and the creek. Involved in my
thoughts, I passed through an undifferentiated gray wood,
gray trunks of generic trees, gray sky, gray of last year's
foliage rotting on the forest floor.

A mile out, on the highest point of the ridge, I heard
the skunk. The funny little animal voice summoned me
into the world like the sudden focusing of a lens. I looked
around me, as though I had just been plopped down from
outer space. The sky had not been gray, but a serene early-
spring ice-blue. The trees wore no gray at all, though I
looked for it, hard, wanting to justify the misty perceptions of the preceding moments. The silvery steel of the
beeches came closest. Everything else shone brown and
red-brown and red and red-black, animated by the Jacob's-
laddering of nuthatches easing down and creepers scrambling up.

The skunk was thirty feet away, singing. I decided to
test my luck. I moved closer, then closer, to a big log,
which seemed a sort of magic barrier. Something told me
she would suffer me to sit on the log, which I did, but not
to cross over, which I did not. The skunk was building a
nest against a fallen maple, on the ridgepole of the forest,
close to water, far from the farm dogs, high, dry, riddled
with light. What I heard the night before as mumbling
and chuckling was clearly singing. The skunk sang as she
built her nest in paradise.

The song was without meter. It had rhythm, I suppose, but one as complex and random as rainfall. The pitch wandered and rambled. It was contemplative, improvisational, the work of a monk rather than a performer. If you weren't actually looking at the animal, you could mistake the sound for water falling over stones.

Of course she knew I was there, listening. She had invited me.

If I was going to come to the magic barrier on one side, so was she on the other. She walked over to my log, reared up on her hind legs, let herself down so her paws were resting on it. I felt them touch, felt her small weight change the alignment of the log. She stared at me for a moment—not singing then, but dead silent—then dropped back to all fours, and went about her business, which was, I see now, as much singing as building. When it was time for me to go, I made a great stir, so she would remember I was there, so she would not be taken by surprise. She barely stopped scuffling and rooting as I eased back down the side of the ridge.

I did not ask myself at the time what I would have done if she had not stopped at the far end of my log, if she had kept on coming. Run like hell, I suppose. Nor did I stop then to wonder what the *meaning* of it all might be. It seemed so much like an acquisition, a treasure yielded by the world, that the *having* was enough, and I didn't give a thought for meaning. And perhaps I was right. Any mystic will tell you that the meaning of a vision is the experience of the vision. Explanation, however canny, lies outside vision. It is given to us less to understand than to see, less to know than to love.

My bookish and apparently somewhat urban affect causes people to be surprised that I know about nature. When they ask how I happen to know so many wild things and so much of their histories, I generally say that I studied them, which is the way most people find out about most things. However reasonable this answer is, it is for the most part a lie, if one that makes more sense than the truth. The truth is that I don't know how I learned these things, have no recollection of not knowing them, and when I do remember the moment of a discovery, it is easiest to describe it in terms of mystical apprehension. Bird, beast, flower, simply announced their names to me at first sight. I said, *trillium,* to myself the first time I stumbled on their blooms littering a wooded hill in Goodyear Heights Metropolitan Park. I know I had never seen them before. It is unlikely that anyone I knew would have had the faintest idea what they were, beyond, "flower."

The first time I heard the towhee kicking in the scrub behind my father's house, I knew what it was. I knew *that* was the sort of place where such a bird would be found. I was very young, four or five, and it wouldn't have occurred to anyone to tell me all these details, and I wouldn't have forgotten the telling if they had. One might say I had seen these things in a book, and recalled them upon visual confirmation. I say not, though the point is now unprovable.

This experience is one of the reasons I am a confirmed Platonist. I knew things, mostly natural things, I had no business knowing. My explanation is that I knew them because I loved them, and wanted their company so badly. The doors of creation simply opened, and I walked in, or they walked out—however such matters work. I have wanted other things since, and the doors of creation have *not* opened, but one must not be greedy. One must expect such a thing only once or twice. Things come to those who need them. In Eden all things come, always. In this realm, some things come, sometimes, and one may have used up all one's blessings before one discovers what is happening, before one thinks to save the magic for things one might want more deeply, more desperately, later on. In any case, no human can see wild things except through their willingness to be seen. It is a boon granted. Ezra Pound writes, "What thou lovest well remains to thee." I add a corollary: "What thou lovest well awaits thee."

The best illustration of this in my life was a beautiful May morning when I was a student at Hiram College. My roommate and his friends were all biology majors, and the vertebrate zoology class was deeply into birds at the moment. Every morn would see him rising early, meeting his friends, strolling through the woods, identifying, identifying, arguing over identifications, identifying. I was jealous. I was not used to people knowing things I didn't. Birding has become such an important part of my life that it is amazing to recount that there was a time before I had ever done it, even once, and the hour before that May morning was it. But I decided to creep out after the vertebrate class. I took my gigantic binoculars (hugeness in binoculars indicated ornithological seriousness then, just as smallness does now) to Maddy's Pond, at the edge of the college playing fields.

It was as though the birds had been lying in wait for me. They had heard my longing across the treetops, had assembled to assuage—or rather to whet—it. In the space of twenty minutes I saw the myrtle warbler, the green

heron, several pairs of bluebirds nesting in trees that overhung the pond, that fluttered out periodically to gather
insects, the shocking blueness of their backs jangling the
jade green of the miraculous waters. Mallards. A wood
duck. Indigo buntings. Rose-breasted grosbeak. I'd never
seen any of them before, except the mallards in park ponds.
But I knew them all, instantly. I said their names aloud
and wrote them down in a notebook with the date beside
them, as I had watched my roommate do. Then I sat back
in the ferns as one stricken. I had gone out to catch up
with the experts, but now they could go to hell. I'd hit the
mother lode all by myself. To this day that one will make
any list of the ten most wonderful mornings of my life,
not just because I had seen beautiful birds, but because
I knew then that I *could* see them. They were not just for
the bio boys. They were not just for someone else, someone officially entitled. They would come to me. Perhaps
they *preferred* to come to me, for I was a writer. I could
put them in a poem. That May morning filled me with
lasting, overwhelming hunger, a longing like the greed of
a miser, for more, and still *more*. The hunger was for birds
then. As I write so many years later, it is for other things,
but the feel of it is the same, desperate and sweet at once,
so long enduring it is part of my identity now. I would
not know who I was if I were fully satisfied.

～

We have been driving all day, past one site that looks pretty
much like another, nothing in the wake of nothing. The
map says we have arrived at a reservoir in Oklahoma,

shining flat silver under a flat evening sky. The road has been long, the destination debated and unsure. It is one of those times when you wonder why you closed your own door behind you, and set out.

Fed up with my traveling companions (and they, I sense, with me), I elect to take my cot outside and sleep under the stars. I mention that to them—"sleeping under the stars"—so they don't take offense at my leap to solitude. Like a caddis fly larva, I subside into my sleeping bag and sleep. Around us twinkle the lights of threescore other lakeside campsites, as crowded as houses in a suburb. There will be no stars. I doze off to the hum of radios.

One sleeping outside awakens when the sun does. The exposed tip of my nose aches with cold. I notice a certain strangeness in the light long before it occurs to me to stick my head out of the sleeping bag to look. There *is* an extra brightness to things, a shade of organic silver that I don't believe is produced by dawn glancing off the reservoir walls.

The lakeshore, the grass, the gravel, our tent, all the tents and all the trailers shimmer with silver, not metallic, but living silver, shivering like the garments of dancers, one color from horizon to horizon. I focus and see that the silver is made of tens of millions of mayflies, vibrating their transparent wings in the dawn breeze, emerging from their larval stage in the lake. My sleeping bag bristles with new life. The legs of my cot are pronged and studded with jelling mayflies.

The sun mounts, their wings dry, and in silver clouds they lift off and depart, almost silent, wave after wave. I feel the weight on my sleeping bag diminish minutely as the insects leap into the air. The last battalions are still launching when my friends awake. I point to the ebbing tide of mayflies. They agree it must have been a beautiful sight.

We crush thousands breaking camp, packing, taking to the dusty road.

❧

The forest is water standing upright. Trees are columns of water, winding stairs by which rain climbs back to cloud. The flowers breathe out moisture. The birds enclose their little oceans in their hearts.

Early May. Last season's grasshopper eggs hatch in disturbing abundance. The roadside quakes with them. The sound of them leaping away from my shoes is the sound of hail, the little drums of exoskeletons beating in grass and against the wet stones. They are all the same size and, from my eyes' perspective of about five feet over the path, the same color, a blackish brown brightening over into yellow when one of them spreads its wings. No grasshopper is large this early, the entire previous generation having perished last winter.

The prophet Joel thunders, *For a nation is come upon my land, strong, and without number, whose teeth are the teeth of a lion, and he hath the cheek teeth of a great lion. He hath laid my vine waste, and barked my fig tree: he hath made it clean bare, and cast it away; the branches thereof are made white. . . . The field is wasted, the land mourneth; for the corn is wasted; the new wine is dried up, the oil languisheth. . . . Like the noise of chariots on the tops of mountains shall they leap, like the noise of a flame of fire that devoureth the stubble, as a strong people set in battle array . . . the earth shall quake before them; the heavens shall tremble: the sun and the moon shall be dark and the stars shall withdraw their shining.* Joel speaks of the locust, which is the grasshopper in migratory mode. In desert lands, this is no exaggeration. The chitinous tattoo at my feet would require only a few levels of magnification.

The grasshoppers stay with me far up the mountain. Grasshoppers are not abundant citizens either of the deep forest or of the heights, but perhaps the foliage is so new and thin they do not realize that's where they are. Perhaps the press of their numbers in the lowlands is so great they have no choice.

Wild iris lines the path, or did so before last night's torrential rains. Now they're downtrodden, bedraggled, flowers in a myth weeping for a wounded god. I do not know what they are until I lift their injured faces up to mine. Tiny purple-black moths flutter up from the iris beds, mistakable for bits of rotting damp bark.

The deluge that steamrolled the irises polished the sky. Clouds fly white and silver and purple-gray under cobalt of immaculate purity. I grope for appropriate words.

The question is, *What to Do with the Abundance?*

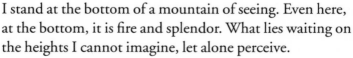

I stand at the bottom of a mountain of seeing. Even here, at the bottom, it is fire and splendor. What lies waiting on the heights I cannot imagine, let alone perceive.

Blue. Blue. Blue. Surely fire and blue.

If skill at expression fails the blue of the storm-washed sky, it does no better with the green of the mountains, sap-swollen, luminous, living emerald spread on the sawteeth

of the Blue Ridge. At one point the deep cut of Bent
Creek Gap flows out of eyeshot, a turbulent jade sea. Farther up the path opens a still greater valley, of deeper green,
at the edge of which, just before another range of burning
emerald mountains, the town of Asheville lies like some
Grecian hilltop city sparkling in the light that began the
world. Distance makes beauty. Distance allows me to forget everything I know of that lived-in place, and see purely.

Last night, just before sunset, two great rainbows ended
a string of thunderstorms. The higher was vast and pale,
its feet invisible in the mountains. The lower one was near
and brilliant, one foot apparently in the Winn-Dixie
parking lot, the other at the mouth of my own street. I'd
never seen one so bright, a fire in the middle of the air.
Anyone could read the signs. Anyone could feel the rainbows linger into night, subtler, paler, lit by stars, and only
the innocent or the mad could see them.

Trillium and dogwood whiten the slopes. Cool palms
of bloodroot, a little after flowering time, clap in the greenish shadows. Sapsuckers scream in the tulip-poplars, under
a veil of saffron and malachite. It's one of those May days
so beautiful it's hard to know what to look at. It's one of
those May days so beautiful as to cause existential dilemma.
Just as we have determined never to be deceived again
there falls this seraphic loveliness. Two or three days a
year the absolute identity of beauty and truth is provable.
This is one of them. If it were a little less perfect, a little
less aflame we could believe it a fresh deceit. If we reached
up and pulled away the mask of the world we would un-
cover fiercer blue, a blaze of oceanic green, a more central
conflagration.

Some weariness in me wants to turn away, to reject

Beauty now because in a moment it will be gone. I keep looking. Beauty says, *Thank you. In return I shall be as I am forever.* That is its deceit for the day, so transparent as to be forgiven.

I continue to the top of the mountain, where in the thirties someone built a lookout tower. It's a ruin now, its scattered blocks assembled and shattered according to the whim of the last visitor. I make a discipline of passing like the wind. I bump a block, swivel it back to its original posture. In this I am wilder than the animals, who pass as wind because their fathers did, without my passion or my will. I could be home sipping tea. I could be writing a book that would make me famous.

A little beyond, the woods open on a vista of the mountains. Green, as I have said perhaps often enough; still, and yet vibrant, as though this were a sea petrified mid-breaker. I perch on the world's pinnacle and stretch out the hands of my heart. I long to touch everything. I lean against a dogwood, the sudden pressure startling a jay from the topmost branch. I reach back through its mothers and their mothers to the World Before, when the jay was a dinosaur grazing on the blossoms rather than a bird launching out from them. I think if I sit long enough all things will want to touch me back, not only all things that are, but all that ever were. I want to hear the river that carved that quiet valley, the roaring of great beasts mating and dying on its banks. I want to hold between my fingers the father of the bloodroots, the sire of oaks; touch the feathers of the first Screamers among the branches, toothed and clawed but with hearts already wedded to the sky. I want to cling to the mountain this was at the beginning.

Climb down now, stepping sideways because of the trick knee. We grow old.

I know how to do this only in one direction. I say what is, unable to endure knowledge of what will come. To put it another way, I am a voluptuary, not a glutton; I leave the future alone.

Acknowledgments

I must express my gratitude for the opportunity Milkweed Editions has given me to republish *A Sense of the Morning*, allowing it a second life eleven years after its first appearance. This has provided me with the unusual chance to rewrite a book already somewhat in the public ken, now that time has passed and I have come closer to understanding what I really meant when the project was begun. As any writer knows, the process of writing is not of setting down what one knows already, but of discovery. If one knows at the outset what one is going to write, and writes exactly that, then one had best not bother. I myself know nothing until I write it down, or say it to a classroom, and often not even then until it has been said or written several times over.

In the making of this book I am especially grateful to Lilace Mellin, who remembered and cherished *A Sense of the Morning* when even I, out of a sense of despair for its future, had almost forgotten it. I wish to thank Susan Rhew and Elton Glaser, who taught me a little about the making of books.

DAVID BRENDAN HOPES is a professor of literature and language, humanities, and creative writing at the University of North Carolina at Asheville. He holds a Ph.D. from Syracuse University and has been awarded several prizes for poetry, fiction, and playwriting, including the Juniper Prize and the Saxifrage Prize for his volume of poems, *The Glacier's Daughters*. His essays have appeared in the *New Yorker, Audubon, Bird Watcher's Digest,* and *Conservation,* among other publications. He is a founder and coeditor of the *Asheville Poetry Review* and is a member of the Asheville National Poetry Slam Team. He began painting in the early nineties and since 1994 has run Urthona Gallery in downtown Asheville.

More Books on The World As Home
from Milkweed Editions

To order books or for more information,
contact Milkweed at (800) 520-6455
or visit our website (www.milkweed.org).

Brown Dog of the Yaak:
Essays on Art and Activism
Rick Bass

Boundary Waters:
The Grace of the Wild
Paul Gruchow

Grass Roots:
The Universe of Home
Paul Gruchow

The Necessity of Empty Places
Paul Gruchow

Taking Care:
Thoughts on Storytelling and Belief
William Kittredge

Ecology of a Cracker Childhood
Janisse Ray

The Dream of the Marsh Wren:
Writing As Reciprocal Creation
Pattiann Rogers

The Country of Language
Scott Russell Sanders

The Book of the Tongass
Edited by Carolyn Servid and Donald Snow

Homestead
Annick Smith

Testimony:
Writers of the West Speak On Behalf of Utah Wilderness
Compiled by Stephen Trimble and Terry Tempest Williams

Other books of interest to The World As Home reader

ESSAYS

The Heart Can Be Filled Anywhere on Earth:
Minneota, Minnesota
Bill Holm

Shedding Life:
Disease, Politics, and Other Human Conditions
Miroslav Holub

CHILDREN'S NOVELS

No Place
Kay Haugaard

The Monkey Thief
Aileen Kilgore Henderson

Treasure of Panther Peak
Aileen Kilgore Henderson

The Dog with Golden Eyes
Frances Wilbur

ANTHOLOGIES

Sacred Ground:
Writings about Home
Edited by Barbara Bonner

Verse and Universe:
Poems about Science and Mathematics
Edited by Kurt Brown

POETRY

Boxelder Bug Variations
Bill Holm

Butterfly Effect
Harry Humes

Eating Bread and Honey
Pattiann Rogers

Firekeeper:
New and Selected Poems
Pattiann Rogers

THE WORLD AS HOME, the nonfiction publishing program of Milkweed Editions, is dedicated to exploring our relationship to the natural world. Not espousing any particular environmentalist or political agenda, these books are a forum for distinctive literary writing that not only alerts the reader to vital issues but offers personal testimonies to living harmoniously with other species in urban, rural, and wilderness communities.

Milkweed Editions publishes with the intention of making a humane impact on society, in the belief that literature is a transformative art uniquely able to convey the essential experiences of the human heart and spirit. To that end, Milkweed publishes distinctive voices of literary merit in handsomely designed, visually dynamic books, exploring the ethical, cultural, and esthetic issues that free societies need continually to address. Milkweed Editions is a not-for-profit press.

Interior design by Donna Burch
Typeset in Adobe Garamond
by Stanton Publication Services Inc.
Printed on acid-free, recycled
55# Phoenix Opaque Natural paper
by Edwards Brothers